CW00421159

# NOEL EDMONDS

# Noel Edmonds
## The Unauthorised Biography

*Alison Bowyer*

*Virgin*

## Acknowledgements

The author wishes to thank Paul Scott, Andy, Judith Chilcote, Paul Burnett, David Jensen, Dave Christian, Mike Smith, Janet Coare, Ed Straw, Stephen Taylor, Peter McMaster, Ray McGuirk, Derek James and all the people who contributed to this book.

First Published in Great Britain by
Virgin Publishing Ltd
Thames Wharf Studios
Rainville Road
London W6 9HT

A catalogue record for this book is available from the British Library.

ISBN 1 85227 788 2

Typeset by TW Typesetting, Plymouth, Devon

Printed by Creative Print and Design (Wales), Ebbw Vale

# Contents

# 1 Party Politics

WHEN NOEL EDMONDS boarded his Squirrel helicopter to make the ninety-minute flight from London to his Devon estate on a cold winter's day in January 1998, he knew his career hung in the balance.

The nation's most popular television presenter had just embarked on a high-stakes game of brinkmanship that could have seen his 29-year career with the BBC end in the sack. Edmonds, the all-smiling frontman of the Corporation's flagship show, had walked out of an afternoon planning meeting of the following night's *Noel's House Party* because the episode was not up to scratch. Now at the age of 49, the man who began his BBC life as a Radio 1 DJ, before bringing gunge tanks, Mr Blobby and those jumpers to an audience of up to 15 million viewers, was ready to think the unthinkable and pull *House Party* with just 24 hours' notice.

The strategy, far from resulting in dismissal and disapproval, was to confirm Edmonds as the most powerful presenter ever to grace British television. He is the man whose personality is the key to the show that, above all others – news, costume drama, soaps and sport – is thought by the BBC mandarins to be the most important in their schedules. Edmonds, who doesn't sing, dance or act, has amassed an estimated £20 million fortune primarily from the skill of looking comfortable on live TV. And it was for this talent that, after frenzied negotiations at the very highest levels of the BBC, the Corporation unprecedentedly caved in to their brightest star.

The threat had not been an idle one. At 7 p.m. the following night, instead of walking out in front of the cameras at London's Television Centre, Noel was 200 miles away in his local pub with his wife, Helen. The BBC plugged the gap by repeating *The Best of Noel's House Party*. Edmonds later described the experience as 'a very dark moment'. Tellingly, however, he was to add, 'I like to think I wouldn't have been unemployable.' It is unlikely he would have been out of work for long. At London's Gray's Inn Road, ITV's Network Centre had eyed *House Party* jealously, and, despite a fall from a peak of 15 million viewers to closer to 8 million, Edmonds could have expected at least to match his £8 million BBC contract with their biggest rivals.

Those close to the star have few doubts he would have made the move to commercial television if his gamble had not succeeded. But sources around Edmonds confess there were times during the standoff when he struggled to hold his nerve. 'The implications if it all went wrong were not lost on Noel,' said a colleague. 'But Noel was adamant that he wasn't prepared to let the standards of the show slip.'

By the following Monday, the BBC were announcing that they had kissed and made up. A weekly budget of £300,000 was promised; better guest stars were to be brought in; extra scriptwriters were allocated and the set improved. Edmonds had won the battle.

The way the BBC caved in to him came as a surprise to many in the industry, but not to those who know the star well. For one thing, Edmonds' policy had always been not to fight a battle he didn't believe he could win; and, secondly, as Noel's former promotions executive Derek James says, 'Everybody at the BBC always treated him as if he could walk on water.'

James, who knew and worked with Edmonds for more than four years, reveals, 'I've always been of the opinion that, even back in his radio days, they were all frightened of him.' Edmonds' position is apparently unassailable, says

James, because he is one of the very few big-hitters left in light entertainment. In the battle with the management there was only ever going to be one winner. James observes, 'The standards of *House Party* had been falling, but nobody has the guts to tell Noel what he should do. He has always surrounded himself with people who say yes to him.'

Within the highest echelons of the BBC, Edmonds has long enjoyed the support of Alan Yentob, the director of television at Broadcasting House. When Yentob became controller of BBC1 in 1993, he described *Noel's House Party* as the Corporation's most important show. The two are, if not friends, at least friendly. Yentob, who has a home in the West Country near to where Edmonds lives, has been given lifts to London in Edmonds' private helicopter.

Edmonds has enjoyed the longest run of any entertainer in the prime early-Saturday-evening slot. Before *House Party*, he did a couple of years of *The Noel Edmonds Saturday Roadshow*, and prior to that *The Late, Late Breakfast Show*, which ran for six years. He has also presented *Swap Shop* and *Telly Addicts*.

But even so, Derek James admits to having a slight worry that maybe Edmonds had this time pushed the BBC too far. He says, 'When he pulled the show like that I wouldn't have been at all surprised if it had been the end of him presenting *House Party*. I suppose the BBC just fear being without him.'

The culture of fear is so pervasive within the Corporation, say insiders, that few will dare to speak out. New ideas are stifled by an all-consuming bureaucracy and senior executives survive by milking tried-and-tested ideas and names for fear of failure. It is against this background that Edmonds has thrived. Nobody has emerged who could hope to wrestle the Saturday-night prime-time slot from him.

'Nobody wants to be in the firing line,' says Derek James, 'so it's safer for an employee to say, "OK, the audience figures are down for *House Party*, but we know the format works, let's go on with it." There aren't enough people who are creating something new, so Noel has the BBC over a barrel.'

Indeed, Edmonds remains such a prime commodity at the BBC that negotiations over the dispute went as far as director general John Birt. The Head of Entertainment, Paul Jackson, was sidelined in the row after clashing with Edmonds over budget cuts for *House Party*. Protracted talks aimed at a conciliation were hammered out in the rather faceless office, in a fourth-floor annexe of London's Broadcasting House, occupied by the Corporation's number three, chief executive of BBC Broadcast, Will Wyatt. His intervention with Yentob was to be the pivotal element in resolving the row.

But the very public falling-out was not the first time Edmonds had clashed with his masters.

Indeed, two years before, almost to the day, he reportedly threatened to scrap *House Party* after the BBC demanded his company, Unique Television, contribute £250,000 towards production costs. They were adamant the star should foot part of the filming bill because of the large sums of money he earns from business ventures associated with the programme, such as Mr Blobby theme parks. The Crinkley Bottom spin-offs make him millions of pounds every year, with Mr Blobby alone netting him £1.9 million.

Although £250,000 represented a small part of the £8.8 million cost per series, Edmonds was determined to fight it all the way, and, with 'helpful' stories in the press hinting, once more, that Edmonds might jump ship to ITV, things were smoothed over and the show went on.

And two years before that there had apparently been yet another ultimatum from Edmonds, this time a 24-hour one: either deliver a deal to his liking, or he would defect to ITV.

The star's intermittent quarrels with the BBC are well known among people who have worked closely with him. Andrew Dixon, whom Edmonds hired as his marketing consultant in the early 1990s, recalls, 'He's fought with the

BBC on and off for years. When I was with him and tried to represent him he was fighting with them then. I've seen Noel walk out of meetings. That's what he would do. Half the thing with Noel is knowing how to handle him and it's true he's got a big ego.'

And, says Dixon, Noel has never been afraid to stand up for himself when he feels the need. It's a side of him the public don't see. 'I've seen him when he's about to go on stage, either as a presenter of an awards ceremony or to do his own show, and he is absolutely seething and swearing at everybody under the sun,' Dixon recalls. 'He's had a row with his wife Helen and he's told some producer to go fuck himself and he's got two minutes to be on the stage and he'll still be in the wings effing and blinding. And then he'd open the door, pull back the curtain, go out on stage and you would never have guessed it. It was almost as if he needed it to psyche himself up.'

Speculation within the corridors of power at the BBC is that those in the highest places would not easily forgive Edmonds his humbling of them. But, as one senior source admits, 'While he remains popular with audiences he is holding a winning hand.' The words, whilst acknowledging the star's power, nonetheless alluded to a far greater influence: that of the television viewer. And it would indeed be the public who would in time sound the death knell for the show by voting with their TV remote controls and switching off.

But despite the fact that some undoubtedly think Edmonds is a prima donna, there are others who admire him for the way he stands up to the merciless bureaucracy and budget slashing which epitomises the BBC.

Mike Smith, Edmonds' copresenter on *The Late, Late Breakfast Show*, knows him better than most, but even he was shocked by the star's decision to pull the show. 'I was surprised that his temperament took him that far,' says Smith. 'I always regarded him as less of a hothead than me. I've had my frustrating times with the BBC over budget cuts and things not being as they should be, and I tend to be very upfront and have arguments with them about it. I never thought Noel would go that far, but it's understandable because some of the budget cuts they went through have been quite atrocious.

'The old saying is that you can cut the budget as much as you like, but, as soon as it creeps under the studio door and starts to show on the air, that's when you have to say something.'

At the time of *The Late, Late Breakfast Show* in the late 1980s, Edmonds wasn't the powerful and influential figure he is today. Smith explains: 'Noel wasn't an independent producer then. The show was very much an in-house BBC show and we were both freelance employees of the BBC. Noel was getting £4,000 a show and I was on £1,000 a show. That was the gulf. And then as years have gone by his fee has gone up and up. It's very difficult to extract basic fees now from contracts because he has so many things written into his contract and there are so many independent things, merchandising rights, that his total take for a year is unknown till maybe two years later, when all the merchandising royalties have come in.

'It is debatable whether he owns the format to *House Party*. I would say that as part of his most recent contract negotiations, the ones he did with Alan Yentob a few years ago, the BBC probably gave up some rights to things. I wouldn't say that he owns the whole format. I know that, for instance, with things like the Gotchas, they are still, I believe, paying a royalty to Peter Dulay, the man who produced *Candid Camera*. I used to do Gotchas on *The Late, Late Breakfast Show* and we used to have to use Dulay as a consultant – that was part of the deal. There are all sorts of things that spin off, but basically I would say that to stand there on Saturday night Noel probably received a basic fee of £25,000, and he's worked himself up over the years to that. He's been there a long time.

'My only worry about Noel in all of this is that he's never

worked anywhere else other than the BBC. He doesn't really know what life is like beyond the BBC. He's always been very clever. At contract-negotiation time you'll always see there's a story planted in the press that says Noel is about to be poached by ITV. And it's not always the truth. He's very, very clever at manipulation.'

'Clever' is a word that crops up a lot when people talk about Edmonds. Derek James says, 'Noel is very clever at live television and he's very good at what he does. He's come a long way and he's done very well for himself, but I think you have to remember that, those you tread on on the way up, you might one day meet on the way down. Noel likes to get his own way. In a way I don't suppose he's different from lots of business people. But I must admit that for the last year or two I've thought the bubble's going to burst. There's no doubt about it, the ratings were dropping – and knowing Noel as I do the last person to take the blame for that would be him.'

James points to the star's deal making with the BBC as one of the major factors in his success. In 1986, Noel headed for America in the hope of repeating his domestic fame Stateside. His bid for stardom failed, but he learnt a lesson that was to promote him into a new superleague of earners never before seen in British television: it is all to do with control. Noel fronted a series of five one-hour specials for American network ABC. The audacious plan was to knock US chat-show king Johnny Carson off his throne. The scheme inevitably failed, but 38-year-old Noel did not come home without taking a leaf out of Carson's book. The talk-show host had for years owned the rights to his show, making him a multimillionaire in the process. When Noel returned to Britain, he vowed to do the same.

Edmonds says, 'I realised that the only successful people in TV would be those who recognised that it was just a small part of the leisure industry.' He owned the intellectual copyright on all aspects of *House Party*, apart from the fifty-fifty deal with the BBC on Mr Blobby, and his multimillion-pound business interests make him unique among TV stars.

He went from being the first superstar disc jockey to the highest-paid TV entertainer. He insists he doesn't like comparisons with his Saturday-night rival Cilla Black, saying, 'I am upset by the media's obsession with creating a league table of performers' pay.' But he tellingly adds, 'However, if there is to be a table I would rather be at the Manchester United than the Nottingham Forest end.'

# 2 The First Noel

NOEL ERNEST EDMONDS was born three days before Christmas 1948. His parents, Dudley and Lydia, had waited six years to be blessed with a child, and Christmas that year was especially joyful for the couple. As their first child was due on 25 December they decided to call him Noel. But, in the event, he arrived early.

Theirs had been a wartime wedding, taking place in the autumn of 1942. Dudley Edmonds was a national-service fireman stationed in Giffnock, near Glasgow, when he met and married schoolteacher Lydia Irving. They were both aged 25 when they exchanged vows on 10 October 1942 at St Stephen's Parish Church in Lydia's home town of Carlisle. Their backgrounds were modest: Dudley's father, Ernest Edmonds, worked as an engineer; and Lydia's father, Lawson Irving, was a storeman on the Lancashire North East Railway.

After the war the couple moved south, to Ilford in Essex, where both found jobs as teachers. They were keen to start a family, but Noel wasn't conceived until early spring 1948.

Ilford in those days, as it is today, was a prosperous town with the majority of people working in the City of London, or employed in the light-engineering and electrical industries. The town was, in the main, lower middle class and very Conservative. It hadn't suffered much from bombings during the Blitz, although a few of the older properties had been damaged by V1 and V2 rocket attacks in the dying days of the war.

Home for young Noel and his parents was 29 Clarendon Gardens, a large black-and-white-painted Edwardian terraced house in a quiet residential street on the outskirts of the town. It was considered one of the nicest roads to live in, not least because it looked on to Valentine's Park, a beautiful expanse of gardens and clipped lawns. Most days when the weather allowed it, Noel's mother would push him out in his pram and cross the road to the park. There they would walk around the ornamental gardens and feed the ducks on the pond while Lydia chatted to other young mothers.

Noel was destined to be an only child and his parents concentrated all their energies on him. Psychiatrists agree that only children, and only sons in particular, are likely to be spoilt by their mothers. According to consultant psychiatrist Dr Raj Persaud, their lack of playmates when younger makes them self-sufficient, but never having to compete for parental attention can make them self-centred. Only sons tend to have the highest self-esteem of all children, says Persaud, but they can be poor at initiating and sustaining relationships, so are likely to experience loneliness. Noel bears much of this out. At the age of five he started at Glade Primary School in Clayhall, Ilford. He recalls, 'I remember being shy at school and I didn't make many friends. As an only child I wasn't used to being natural with other children. My parents were never interested in having any more children and they poured all their resources into me. And that's a real bugger: it puts a hell of an obligation on you.'

Being a sole child was a mixed blessing for Noel. While he missed out on the companionship of siblings and had to carry all his parents' hopes and dreams on his shoulders, he also enjoyed the benefits of having his parents to himself. He says, 'Being an only child made me much closer to my parents. I had an extremely good relationship with them and they have always been interested in everything I have done. I was spoilt. Not in material things – they weren't particularly generous with pocket money – but by all the time and love that was lavished on me. In the school holidays I used to help around the house or play on my own. I remember whole weekends when I wouldn't see another kid and was happy to play with my train set or play cricket with my dad. Because he was a headmaster he had the same holidays as me and we often did carpentry or worked on the car together.'

Dudley, whose middle name Noel shared, rose in his profession to become the head teacher of Gearies Boys School, a state secondary modern in Ilford, and a school Dudley was determined his only son would *not* be attending. He and Lydia wanted more for their son than an ordinary secondary-school education could provide. With teachers for parents, there was always going to be pressure on Noel to do well academically and there was a big emphasis on studies and homework. Indeed, the work ethic Noel has carried with him through life was instilled in him at an early age. It stood him in good stead for what was to come.

Even as a young child Noel had a burning ambition to be famous: 'I don't remember feeling lonely as a child, but I used to spend a lot of time by myself building up a dream world. Since there was no one else around, I created my own standards and decided that I was going to be "successful" and that, when I died, my name would appear on the front pages of the newspapers. I became very self-motivated, very self-reliant. I used to dream about what I wanted to achieve. And I can honestly say that all those critical paths in my life have come from a vision of what I wanted.'

Noel learnt early on that hard work brings its own rewards when, in 1960, at the age of eleven, he won a much prized scholarship to Brentwood School, a direct-grant grammar considered to be the top school in Essex. The attention that his parents had made sure Noel gave to his studies had paid off and, with the chance of the superior education that Brentwood offered, Noel had earned himself a huge leg-up in the world.

The year Noel started at Brentwood, John F Kennedy was on the brink of becoming President of the United States. In Britain, MPs were busy trying to ban teddy boys and gave an unopposed second reading to a bill to curb their behaviour. They were also trying to ban publication of DH Lawrence's novel *Lady Chatterley's Lover* under ancient obscenity laws, a test case that resulted in the book being published for the first time in thirty years. At the cinema, Alfred Hitchcock's *Psycho* was the film to see, and the world mourned when movie star Clark Gable died of a heart attack aged 59. Royal fever hit the country with the birth of Prince Andrew and the marriage of his aunt, Princess Margaret, to commoner Antony Armstrong-Jones.

Arriving at Brentwood, where Home Secretary Jack Straw was a fellow pupil, was a defining moment in Noel's life, for the pupils were, by and large, the sons of well-off lawyers, bankers and accountants who expected only one thing from their lives: success. Their financially comfortable parents had been able to pay for them to go to the expensive Brentwood Preparatory School and, being from similar backgrounds and having known each other from the age of seven, the boys formed something of a clique.

Noel's father, while a respectable headmaster, was not rich, and at Brentwood there was a certain 'us and them' attitude towards boys like Noel who entered the school from the state sector. Nothing was actually said, but the message was nonetheless there: 'You are not one of us.'

Starting a new school is a daunting enough prospect for any child without this extra pressure that Noel had to face. How he coped with the situation showed a remarkable astuteness and is indicative of the clever way he has managed his career ever since. At the tender age of eleven he was already canny enough and shrewd enough to take the situation he found himself in and turn it to his advantage. He quickly realised that the only way to thrive in such an atmosphere was not simply to become 'one of them' but to be the best 'one of them'. He had to gain the respect of his peers. The shyness that had dogged his primary-school days was not evident at Brentwood.

It was at Brentwood that he learnt the skill of people manipulation which was to prove so important to him in later life. Noel saw that a tall, dark-haired boy named Chris Fone seemed to be the most liked and respected in his class. He was the one who made the others laugh and he was clearly the most popular. Noel set out to steal the boy's crown as class clown by beating him at his own game. Whether it was sheer cynical game playing or a natural talent at winning that he didn't even realise he had, Noel's ploy worked. The other boys noticed him. And so cleverly and charmingly did he do it that even the boy whose glory he stole didn't hold it against him. Indeed, not only did the boy not dislike him for it but the two became firm friends.

Fone recalls: 'Before Noel arrived at Brentwood School I had been the form joker, the clown. Then Noel came and he was very competitive. He had to be top dog and I just rolled over and put all four legs in the air and said, "OK, I submit." I joined the bridge club and he had to be better than me. His mum coached him! That competitiveness really dominated our relationship, both as boys and as men.'

Noel's time at Brentwood was not particularly happy, but it helped motivate him in life. 'I was just medium at everything and I was completely overawed by the people who were seriously good at O levels and A levels,' he said. 'The fact that my schooldays were totally undistinguished bothered me. I was obsessed by what I thought was my very obvious lack of star quality. I knew that I would struggle at whatever I decided to do. The horror of school for me was the anonymity of being in the middle of 800 boys. If I analyse it, I think my drive came from the wish not to be anonymous.' The way he handled his early days at Brentwood shows that even at that young age Noel Edmonds was not someone who could be easily ignored. He made his presence felt at the outset and, as Chris Fone wryly remarks, 'We had Noel impacted upon our lives.'

Despite what Noel says about being only medium at everything, he was, according to his schoolfriends, an exceptional all-rounder. He was intelligent, sporty and good-looking, and he breezed into Brentwood as the life and soul of the party. He set out to prove to his school chums, as he was later to prove to his colleagues in the show-business world, that he could be the best at whatever he chose to do.

Noel quickly settled in to life at Brentwood and before long it was as if he had always been there. He enjoyed his newly won position as class clown but was far too sensible to risk blowing the chances he had been given by getting into any serious trouble. Noel knew he was lucky to be at Brentwood and realised the school's strict emphasis on academic achievement would stand him in good stead in the future. And of course he had the work ethic. Fone, who now runs his own sound-system installation company, explains, 'Noel was always the joker and he had a good sense of humour but he was too much of a goody-goody to get into trouble. He was a very responsible sort of chap.'

Some boys may have disliked Noel for this, and there was something else going against him, too. There was a disquieting feeling among the other boys that Noel might be perhaps just a tad too clever. They remember him being generally popular, but, in the age-old tradition of school life, his intellect was the subject of a certain amount of jealousy and resentment. But there was also another, darker reason why not everyone liked Noel – a reason future victims of his now-legendary pranks would understand only too well. Fone explains: 'If Noel did get up people's noses it was because a lot of his humour was at other people's expense.' No one likes to be made a fool of and, unlike now, when Noel proudly boasts that his pranks are never designed to hurt people's feelings, as a schoolboy he hadn't honed his sense of humour so carefully and people did get wounded.

When they knew Noel had got into Brentwood, his parents sold the house in Ilford and bought a new home in

Gidea Park, a smart new suburb of Romford. The whole area around their old home in Clarendon Gardens was gradually changing as the large Edwardian houses were divided into flats. Gidea Park was an exciting and attractive new development. It had been built as a separate estate, with model houses set in a garden suburb. The area was more prosperous than where the Edmonds had lived before, and was very middle class. While slightly smaller than their old house, 9 Risebridge Road was semidetached and very pretty, with cherry trees in the front garden. It backed on to open heathland, complete with a golf course which Noel's golf-crazy mother quickly made use of.

During his years at Brentwood, Noel formed a friendship with Chris Fone which was to last for more than twenty years. The two were in the same house at school, South House, and were also neighbours. They often made the journey to and from school together on the number 251 bus. Once Fone had 'rolled over and submitted', they became close, and Noel was not an easy person to get close to. Fone says, 'Noel is very much a people person but I think the difference is that it is on his terms. The determined streak is never far away.'

During their friendship, Noel would often confide in Chris about the trouble with being an only child. Dudley and Lydia had been delighted when their son passed the scholarship exam to Brentwood and were determined that his excellent progress shouldn't stop there. Chris Fone says, 'Being the only son of a couple of teachers probably had a large effect on Noel. I think as much as anything it was an overdoting mother determined that her son would be the best. His father was a very nice, kind chap, but, in my opinion, his mother was too dominant. Noel felt it was a huge responsibility to live up to their expectations. He confided in me many times that he wished they weren't so strict with him.' Edmonds admits that it is only now that he is a father himself that he realises just how much he missed out on by not having brothers and sisters.

Neighbours in Risebridge Road remember Noel as a somewhat solitary youngster. Joyce Gray, who lived three doors away, recalls, 'He was lonely, not allowed to be very friendly at all. His father made him do plenty of schoolwork, kept his nose to the grindstone. I used to see a bit of his mother and she wasn't one of the easiest people, a bit snobby. Rather fancied things.' Even Noel used to take the mickey out of his mother, calling her 'Lydia from Gidea'. He was to later remark to a friend, 'Oh, Mum would love to be a duchess.'

Chris Fone confirms much of this, adding, 'It must have been hard having a mother like his. There would never be a girl good enough for him. I know what people mean about Lydia having snobbish pretensions, but it depends where one is coming from. I think she had extremely middle-class values and she saw that as a very good thing. She was determined that her son would have the best of whatever she could provide.'

But, whatever those who knew her considered Lydia Edmonds' shortcomings to be, no one was in any doubt that she absolutely loved and adored her son. And he in turn loved and adored her. Noel has always believed in the importance of family and rather touchingly once described him and his parents as being 'like a triangle'. Noel got on well with his parents, particularly his father, and the two of them would spend hours tinkering with go-karts and later building their own car together. Edmonds says, 'I think I'll be doing well if I get my kids to a point where it would hurt them to upset me, because that's how I felt about my parents. It mattered that they approved of what I did. I never wanted to upset them. They taught me the old-fashioned values like discipline, respecting one's elders, being grateful for what you've got.'

During the school vacations the family would holiday in Weymouth, where Noel made his first public appearance at the age of nine, in a junior talent show at the Weymouth Pavilion. 'I was strolling along the pier with my mum and dad when we saw the talent show taking place and they entered me,' recalled Noel. 'I recited "The Postman Cometh". I've no memories of the occasion but my mum took a photograph of me and I'm reminded of it every time she gets the picture out and says to people, "This was his first public performance." It never fails to embarrass me.' Other holidays were spent in the Lake District with Noel's Aunt Poll, who is now in her late eighties and to whom Noel is devoted to this day. Townie Noel remembers being amazed that he could walk down the lane near her house and not get flattened by a car. The Lakes remains one of his favourite places.

It was this close bond with his family that helped Noel cope with his first real knock. At the age of fifteen, he was struck down by a serious illness that was to change his life for ever. He developed a serious eye disease which threatened to rob him of his sight. For a short but unbelievably frightening time, it really seemed to Noel and his parents that he might go blind. Worried doctors put him on a course of strong steroids to treat the illness and, although they managed to save his sight, the treatment caused him distressing side effects. They made him painfully bloated and overweight at a crucial stage in his adolescence. Any teenager who has suffered from weight problems or acne knows the embarrassment such cruel afflictions bring. Fifteen is just the age when you are discovering the opposite sex and are acutely aware of your appearance. For a handsome youngster like Noel, it was doubly cruel. All his life he had been considered good-looking and full of vitality, but now he was overweight and spotty.

Chris Fone saw at close hand the effect the illness had on his friend. 'It was very sudden,' he explains. 'I remember him being absent from school for a while and when he came back he had changed. He had to have massive amounts of cortisone steroids, which made him fat and rather changed his life. It was a difficult time for him and he is to this day very sensitive about it.'

Noel's illness was cured and in time the side effects caused by the steroids wore off. His metabolism stabilised and his weight returned to normal, but the whole upsetting experience had changed him for ever. He now knew that he couldn't take anything for granted and from then on a more serious side of him was apparent as he knuckled down to the all-important task of planning The Rest Of His Life.

Loyalty, respect and hard work were values taught to him by his parents and all along it had been expected by Dudley and Lydia – and his teachers – that Noel would get a university degree and follow them into teaching. This was not what Noel wanted – in fact the thought horrified him – but he dutifully went through the motions of applying to universities. But what his parents didn't know, and what Noel confided only to Chris Fone, was that he had a very different career in mind for himself. Noel had become increasingly obsessed with pirate radio and had even built himself a makeshift studio in his bedroom. What he really wanted to be was a disc jockey – then a far more unusual job proposition than it would be today.

As far back as he can remember, Noel's heart was set on becoming a DJ. 'All I ever wanted to do was go into radio, even when I was very small,' he says. 'My passion for radio grew from the pirate radio stations that were anchored off the Essex coast. I realised that there was a direction in which I could go. It was the first time I realised I had the power to communicate with people. It's my only gift. I wanted a job that involved me in people's lives, and that was it.' And, importantly, it was the one area of show business that didn't involve getting up on a stage in front of an audience. 'I am basically very shy,' he revealed. 'I tend to be self-conscious and easily embarrassed and I used to be so bad that, when I first got a brochure from Radio Caroline which showed a studio with an engineer watching the disc jockey while he worked, it came as a terrible shock. I seriously thought I might not be able to do it if there was someone else there. It had never occurred to me that I wouldn't be completely alone.'

But the more he thought about it, the more he realised there was no reason why he shouldn't fulfil his dream. He would do whatever it took to make it happen and from then on it was as if Noel was wearing horses' blinkers, so firmly were his sights set on success. While his schoolfriends were out discovering girls, Noel spent his spare time holed up in his bedroom making his own radio programmes, which he would then try out on his father. For many teenage boys it would have proved to be just a passing phase until the attraction of girlfriends and a social life lured them back into the outside world. But Noel was determined. Missing out on the company of the opposite sex and parties was a small price to pay for the success that he knew could be his. He approached this stage in his life as he has approached everything in his career – with 100 per cent commitment.

Chris Fone comments, 'Because he was determined to become numero uno in the field of disc jockeying – and I can remember him even then talking about television – he was a late developer socially. That was contrary to how he had been as a young adolescent. Then he had been very popular with girls when we travelled on the bus. In fact, it was infuriating for the rest of us because he used to spend all his time chatting them up. He was very good-looking and the rest of us didn't get a look-in. The change in him was odd, really. It was as if a point was reached where a part of him was shut down deliberately, and this again demonstrates his single-mindedness. Noel is shy, but his self-belief system is so strong, so complete, that nothing can stop him achieving what he has set his mind to achieving.'

Nothing meant nothing. Not the shocked disapproval of his father when he announced he wouldn't be taking up the university place after all. Not the tears of his mother, who had wanted so much for her son. Noel's parents saw success, in true middle-class terms, as academic success, and initially they were horrified that he wanted to become a disc jockey of all things! The questions were endless: What about his education? Was it all going to be thrown aside now? What was he going to do with his life? What sorts of prospects did disc jockeying hold? Why was he passing up the chance to train for a proper career? Didn't he realise how lucky he was?

Chris Fone remembers the trouble that ensued when Noel, who had always been the perfect son and done his parents' bidding, defied them for the first time. He recalls: 'To start with they were very upset, but eventually they realised that this passion was not going to go away, and then I would say they were supportive.' And Noel himself admits, 'I knew from the age of sixteen that I wanted to be a disc jockey and the crunch came when I told my parents I didn't want to go to university. It was the only patch when we didn't get on well.'

But, after the initial shock had worn off, Lydia didn't have long to wait until her son was to make her prouder than she could ever have believed possible. For, as a DJ on Radio Luxembourg and, later, Radio 1, Noel would become *famous* and she would bathe in the golden glow of his success. As the mother of Noel Edmonds, the famous DJ, Lydia became something of a celebrity herself in Gidea Park. Neighbours in Risebridge Road remember her proudly displaying a photograph of Noel in the sitting-room window, but not facing in for the Edmonds family to view – facing out for passers-by to see. And he would later buy his parents a Rolls-Royce which Lydia would royally drive to Tesco to do her shopping. Bizarrely, Lydia also asked her son for his autograph. 'My first autograph request was from my mum,' Noel admits. 'She said, "If you are going to be as successful as you think, I'd better have your autograph." '

Once he had set his heart on becoming a DJ, Noel got some early practice in by doing voluntary radio work at the Victoria Hospital in Romford. But, in a compromise with his parents, he didn't neglect his schoolwork and passed ten O levels and three A levels at Brentwood, albeit with average grades.

But his young years weren't all about hard work. Apart

from radio, Noel's other big passion was cars – a love that he feels to this day – and he would spend hours in his father's garage souping up old bangers. His first driving experience had been at the age of nine, when he slammed his father's BSA Tourer straight into the garage wall, an incident which he was later to repeat in a far more expensive motor belonging to Mike Smith. Noel says, 'My father was then a relatively impoverished schoolmaster and had lovingly restored this car. I was sitting at the wheel, going, "Brmm brmm," imagining I was leading at Le Mans or somewhere, and had turned on the ignition so that the little red warning light on the dashboard added to my illusion. In my excitement I pressed the starter button, and the car leapt forward, right into the garage wall. My father's first new car was a Ford Anglia 105, but he thought we had all really arrived when we moved up to a Rover 90. This was second-hand but we thought it was fabulous. My father used to do all the maintenance himself, and so I learnt a great deal from him as well as inheriting his interest in motor vehicles.'

Noel had an affinity with all things mechanical and he used to do up go-karts and sell them. When he was fifteen, he bought his first go-kart for £30. He says, 'I was one of the first people to study karting and engine maintenance as a Duke of Edinburgh's Award Scheme subject, at school at Brentwood. The regime there was such that they injected me with education for six days a week and on the seventh day I would poodle around with engines. My father always said to Mum, who was terrified about the whole thing, "There's absolutely no way you can have an accident in a kart. And this practice will be good for Noel's driving in the future." He was quite right. I didn't have an accident; but he managed to roll the kart over and was off work for six weeks.'

Money from the go-karts also helped Noel buy his home music studio and meant that, like his better-off schoolmates, he always had money in his pocket. 'We weren't a wealthy family but I always had my own money,' he says. 'By the time I was seventeen and old enough to have a driving licence, I had bought a Minivan for ninety quid. I gradually did it up and delighted in getting more power out of the engine. I really like a car that is a wolf in sheep's clothing. I had the cylinder head skimmed, fitted a second carburettor and a better exhaust manifold. It was originally a horrible sort of green colour, and I hired a spray gun and changed this to various shades of blue, according to what cans of paint I could scrounge. I then put windows in it, and for this I had to pay some ridiculous sums of money to the Customs and Excise for changing it into an estate car. I drove it to school every day, which was a great pose at the age of seventeen. It had a mattress in the back which was very popular with my friends, but it was far more innocent than it sounds. My mates used to complain about how hard it was sitting in the back of the van when we were all going to the pub, so I put the mattress in.'

As well as selling go-karts at sixteen, Noel had exhibited earlier signs of his money-making abilities. He explains, 'I remember a school trip to Denmark. I traded in oranges and apples on the train to Harwich because everyone opened their packed lunch very quickly and didn't want the fruit. I ended up with a barrow-load of it. Then we had a horrendous North Sea crossing where everyone chucked up, and on the train journey to Copenhagen they were desperate for an orange. I did seriously well out of that. It was making the most of an opportunity.' It was an indication of things to come, but it was to be quite a few years before Noel's love of business and money making would eclipse his love of radio.

Like many teenagers in the 1960s, Noel sent tapes off to dozens of pirate radio stations, including several in America. Most didn't bother to reply. Noel explains, 'When I left school I wanted desperately to try my luck as a disc jockey. It seemed like the perfect escape from the threat of a lifetime of mediocrity. It offered the possibility of fame and glamour without, apparently, the need for formal qualifications.'

But his attempts met bitter disappointment. He had thought his luck was in when, the day before he left school in 1967, he was offered a job on a pirate radio station. He had sent a tape to Radio London, where his hero Tony Windsor was immediately impressed with his style but thought he needed experience. Windsor, a deep-voiced DJ who worked on various pirate radio stations, including the floating station Radio Caroline, arranged for Noel to have a job at Radio 355, which was run by his brother. Noel was overjoyed, but his happiness was short-lived. Within a month, the Marine Offences Bill became law. Pirate radio stations were now outlawed and Radio 355 closed down. An American radio station in Oregon offered Noel an audition and he was shocked to find himself seriously contemplating the journey. Then he came to his senses and realised it was a *bit* too far to go for a job interview.

Noel was desperately disappointed. He had been offered a place at Bristol University but felt that taking it would be like admitting defeat. As a delaying tactic, he got himself a job as a student teacher while he made up his mind what his next move should be. It was at a primary school in Seven Kings, Essex, and Noel hated it. 'I was in a tough school where a lot of the kids were right little horrors,' he recalled. Many of his fellow teachers were completely overrun by their classes, but Noel didn't have far to look for advice on handling unruly pupils. Having a headmaster for a father was a great help. Dudley told his son that if he couldn't establish discipline in his class he would never get anywhere, so Noel quickly learnt how to control the youngsters. The experience, albeit unpleasant at times, taught him how to get on with children – something that would prove useful when he came to host the children's television programme *Swap Shop*.

Then came the call that changed his life. Despite what had happened with the doomed job at Radio 355, fate had determined that it would be Tony Windsor who gave Noel his first big break. Noel was lying under a car when the telephone call that was to change his life came through. It was Sunday 4 August 1968 when his mother's voice came over the intercom that his father had installed in the garage. 'I was working underneath my Mini Jem with my father when my mother said someone called Tony Windsor wanted to talk to me on the phone. The effect on me was literally stunning: I was so excited I got up in such a hurry that I banged my head on the sump. As I slithered out from underneath the car on my back and rubbed the swelling lump on my forehead with an oily hand, I began to tremble with excitement. Somehow I just knew that I was about to be given some very important and exciting news. Tony wanted me to audition for Radio Luxembourg.'

Noel could not believe his luck. Radio Luxembourg was Britain's only commercial radio station, and the fact that it operated from foreign parts and without permission from the authorities only added to its appeal. Until the launch of Radio 1 the year before, if you wanted to listen to the Beatles or the Rolling Stones you listened to Radio Luxembourg, or Fab 208 as it became affectionately known. It was required listening for the pop-loving teenagers of Britain, who would spend hours dedicatedly twiddling the knobs on their radios, trying to coax decent reception from the notoriously weak signal.

Noel admits to being 'absolutely terrified' when he arrived at Radio Luxembourg's London headquarters for his interview, and was even more overwhelmed when he found himself face to face with one of his heroes – DJ Pete Murray. 'I was sitting in the reception area twitching with fear as I waited to be summoned, when Pete suddenly wandered out of the studio and sat down opposite me,' recalls Noel. 'He said I must be there for an audition because he couldn't think of any other reason why I would be looking quite so scared to death. He told me not to be nervous because I would blow it, and not to be too cocky either. He told me to just be myself and wished me good luck.'

Murray's advice gave Edmonds the extra confidence he

needed to see him through the interview, but he had to wait an agonising full month, until 3 October, before he heard that he had got the job. 'Every day seemed like a fortnight,' he admitted. 'I'll never forget the night they announced over the air that I was joining them.' He was due to start at Surrey University the following day on a Human Relations course involving psychology, philosophy and sociology. 'I just threw my education out of the window,' he said.

No one could blame him. It was a fabulous opportunity. Radio Luxembourg was the birthplace of the disc jockey – fast-talking, trendy young men who became as much a part of the culture as the records they were playing. It was inspirational and he was going to be part of it. The heady days of megastardom were just around the corner.

# 3 Fab 208

W HEN RADIO LUXEMBOURG closed down on New Year's Eve 1992, whole generations of British radio listeners were left misty-eyed with nostalgia. Millions had grown up listening to Fab 208, and when it finally closed its doors it was the end of an era. The station, whose fortunes had been slowly declining since the legalisation of commercial radio in 1973, had become a small voice among many. But for decades it was the only voice for young pop fans.

Tony Prince, one of the first disc jockeys to broadcast live from Radio Luxembourg, and a contemporary of Noel's, explains the station's unique appeal. He says, 'The importance of Radio Luxembourg goes way beyond just a pop-music station. Elvis Presley listened to it when he was stationed in Germany. The Beatles heard their first single played for the first time on Radio Luxembourg. It was inspirational. The signal went way beyond the British Isles. We had a huge audience in Eastern Europe and Russia. We were going over the wall long before it came down. For many of those kids it was the only place they could hear Western pop music.'

At its height in the 1960s, 10 million listeners tuned in to Radio Luxembourg. Their biggest audience was on Sunday evenings, when it broadcast the top-twenty hits of the week in an hour-long programme. Free from the restraints of Home Office legislation, Luxembourg was able to enjoy a close and lucrative relationship with advertisers and record companies, many of whom had contracts with the station to plug their records. For years it was the only alternative to the BBC.

In the 1930s, the BBC was ruled with a rod of iron by Lord Reith, a man whose vocabulary didn't include the word 'fun'. Sundays, in particular, were a glum time if you were looking to the radio for entertainment. Reith considered the Sabbath to be a sacred day best devoted to high-minded contemplation, preferably of a godly nature, and ordered that only religious programmes be broadcast. For the millions of British listeners who just wanted to relax and enjoy themselves, Radio Luxembourg proved an oasis.

Its founders, Radio Publicity, who operated from offices in Chancery Lane, London, saw the opportunity for beaming a commercial radio station from France to the British mainland. Broadcasts started from Fecamp, home of Benedictine liqueur, but the French complained about their airwaves being 'polluted by the sound of English' and ordered transmissions to cease. The company heard that a new high-power transmission station in Luxembourg was nearing completion and moved its base there. Radio Luxembourg was launched on 3 December 1933 from the Villa Louvigny within the ancient walls of Luxembourg City, a fact that many of its listeners were happily ignorant of. Sir Cliff Richard, a fan of the station, admits that he didn't even realise Luxembourg was a country. 'I thought it was just a couple of rooms with DJs in,' he says. 'It was years later, when I was actually making records, before I realised it was a country.'

One of the station's earliest, and most notorious, presenters was William Joyce, better known as Lord Haw-Haw. Joyce was given control of the studios during the war by the Germans, and he broadcast hoax propaganda reports of German victories, a crime for which he was later hanged in England. And it was Radio Luxembourg that gave us the Ovaltinies Club, which extolled the virtues of the bedtime drink and brought a visit from a member of the

Luxembourg secret police who thought the Ovaltinies' 'coded messages' meant that spies were at work. Before the war, a survey for the London School of Economics found that the station had twenty times the audience of some BBC programmes.

In the 1950s the station brought rock and roll to the attention of British youth and gained a new audience of young people. It also gave birth to the cult of the disc jockey and launched the careers of Pete Murray, Hughie Green, David Jacobs and Sir Jimmy Savile. In the 1960s, its heyday, it was the training ground for people like David Jensen, Paul Burnett, Tony Prince – and Noel Edmonds.

Noel was a fresh-faced nineteen-year-old when he joined Radio Luxembourg in October 1968. This was the year when students and workers combined to rebel against authority. There were demonstrations in London and Paris, and rock and free love were celebrated. Manfred Mann, Cliff Richard, the Rolling Stones, the Beach Boys, Joe Cocker and Fleetwood Mac all had number-one hit records, and the Beatles held the number-one spot twice, first with 'Lady Madonna' and then with 'Hey, Jude'. The world mourned when civil-rights leader Martin Luther King was assassinated in America. His murderer, James Earl Ray, fled to Britain, where he was arrested in London two months after the brutal killing. Three days before Ray's arrest, millions reeled with the shock of a second assassination: Bobby Kennedy was shot dead. And in London a gangland reign of terror was brought to an end with the arrest of the Kray Twins, Ron and Reggie.

The first record Noel played as a DJ was 'Jesamine' by the Casuals. 'There was no time to be nervous,' he said. 'I was just thrown in and got on with it.' It was his first job but he was immediately earning more money than his father. As headmaster of a secondary school, Dudley Edmonds' annual salary was £2,400. For playing records on the radio, his son was earning £3,500.

But it was soon pretty clear to those who heard him in

action that Noel had a special talent for radio which involved far more than simply being able to spin records. He was, by his own description, 'a personality jock', using the records as mere interludes for a series of skits, running gags, and audience-participation scams. While the other disc jockeys played record after record, stopping only for the news or weather reports, Noel talked to his listeners and invited them to talk back to him. He was the first disc jockey to encourage the audience to become involved in his shows, and he built up an instant rapport with his listeners that amazed many of the people he worked with. With the volume of commercial radio stations around today, it is easy to underestimate Edmonds' influence on the industry, but it was his pioneering style which has been copied so successfully by people like Chris Tarrant and Chris Evans.

Fellow DJ Paul Burnett was already at Radio Luxembourg when Edmonds arrived, and he well remembers the impact he made. He recalls: 'Noel was very new to disc jockeying – I think he'd done some hospital radio before he got there, that was his only prior experience – but he took to it like a fish to water. Most of the time we just played a record, did a few requests or a competition, but Noel was very good at introducing things into his show that would stimulate a response from the audience. Getting audience involvement is not an easy thing to do, but from very early on in his radio career Noel was very, very astute and sharp at that.'

Christine Prince, whose DJ husband Tony worked with Noel in Luxembourg, believes the star was at his very best in those early days. She says, 'Noel was very good. I don't think he was ever better.'

Tony tells how he immediately knew that Noel had a special talent: 'I used to sit there, as indeed did all his colleagues, listening to his type of broadcasting and being thoroughly entertained. And you were aware that this guy was going to be phenomenally successful. We were very close and I remember him saying to me, "I'm not going to be a DJ all my life. I'm just going to use it as a platform." '

Landing the job at Radio Luxembourg had been a marvellous stroke of luck for Noel because it was the most happening radio station of its day. Its informal style and emphasis on pop music made it the perfect place for the young disc jockey to experiment and find his own unique style. Years later, after it closed down, Noel was to describe his time there as the happiest of his life. Burnett explains the station's appeal: 'Radio Luxembourg was, at that time, second only to the BBC in terms of prestige and when you got there you really did think you had *arrived*. And the money was very good because all the fringe benefits were good. We would actually start our working day at about five o'clock in the afternoon and generally socialise until about four in the morning at nightclubs and discos. They were good times: we didn't have responsibilities; we were staff not freelance; we were young with no mortgages and yet getting very good money for our age.'

It certainly wasn't hard work. All Noel had to do was be himself. Burnett says, 'The funny thing about being disc jockeys is that we are not really performers – we are just being ourselves on the air. An element of performance comes into it but basically what you are selling, or projecting, is an exaggerated extension of yourself. That's what the good ones do. You are not hiding behind a mask.'

But Noel's first live broadcast on Luxembourg was very nearly his last. Reading the news bulletin about an outbreak of typhoid that had been sweeping across Italy, he caused hysterics in the studio by solemnly saying, 'The epidemic is believed to have been started by an ice-cream salesman washing his utensils in the Po!' 'I had been so anxious not to make a mistake that I'd read it over to myself a hundred times before I went on air,' he recalled. 'There was immediate uproar in the studio and when I realised what I'd said I got the giggles, too. I went red in the face trying not to laugh out loud and the tears were rolling down my face. There was no way I could read the weather report! I spent the rest of the evening feeling dreadful. I was certain I would be fired.'

Noel shared a flat at 25 Avenue de la Fiancerey with another fresh-faced newcomer, eighteen-year-old Canadian David Jensen. As they were in their teens and the others were in their twenties, the two had decided they would find a place together. It was a very small apartment with the stove in the living room and the bedroom just behind a partition. Jensen recalls, 'Luxembourg was quite an expensive place to live so we pooled our resources and set up a flat together for six of the nine months that he was there. I don't remember the money being good. I remember the last few days of the month especially, eating cold ravioli and counting the francs on the floor to see what we could afford – Paul Burnett must have been on more money than us! It was very much a bachelor pad but it was not too much like *Men Behaving Badly*. Noel was pretty orderly.'

Jensen had been promptly nicknamed 'Kid' by Paul Burnett and the other jocks, and the name stuck. For years afterwards he was known to radio listeners as Kid Jensen, even when he was in his late thirties. Noel managed to escape having his name changed – but only just. His boss, Tony Windsor, wanted him to change his name to the unlikely-sounding 'Randy West'. Edmonds refused – even at school, where everybody had a nickname, Noel had only ever been known as Noel – but the teasing went on. Showing another new recruit, Dave Christian, around the station one day, Windsor pointed to Edmonds and said, 'There is a little boy over in the corner whose name is Randy West, but we don't like it so we are going to change his name to Noel Edmonds.' Noel later remarked, 'Can you imagine me saying, "Hi, I'm Randy," every time I went on air!' And one can only imagine what Lydia Edmonds would have made of her only son being renamed Randy – or the other names that were put forward, such as Noel Van Demon and Noel St Lawrence.

Away from home and doing a job he loved, Noel began to loosen up and enjoy himself. He got on well with the other DJs, many of whom were to remain his friends for years to come. Says Paul Burnett, 'We would be out in Luxembourg for long stretches – that was why it was so good in terms of camaraderie. We all relied on each other socially, and as well as working together we would party together and pretty well do everything together because we were Englishmen in a foreign country.' His colleagues at Radio Luxembourg say Noel's love of practical jokes started there and they should know – they were on the receiving end of most of them. Burnett says, 'Noel certainly wasn't one of those serious types – it was all fun and he turned that to his advantage. I think the seeds to all the setups and the Gotchas were sown in Luxembourg.'

Dave Christian, who lived in the flat above Noel and David Jensen on the Avenue de la Fiancerey, had his patience tried more than once. He says, 'He irritated me all the time. He was a pest. His idea of fun was to take the handle off my door and just leave it hanging there so that, when I came home after doing the 1 a.m.–4 a.m. programme and tried to get into my apartment, the bloody door handle would come off in my hand. When you really want to go to bed and you are tired and it's five o'clock in the morning and the birds are out and the sun is coming up, it is not funny. I would sit on the landing for an hour and a half smoking cigarettes and eventually Noel would let me in. I now work for a radio station called Sunshine which, funnily enough, is right next door to where we all used to live. It is strange walking past it every day and remembering what we got up to. Most of our time was spent wondering when we would get our next meal because we weren't paid very well. It was crap. Me and David Jensen used to share an apartment together at one time and we starved. We lived on a tin of ravioli every day for about six months. We hate it now.'

The pranks Noel played on Dave Christian were nothing compared to the grand scheme he dreamt up for Kid Jensen. It was an elaborate and crazy plan whereby he, Paul Burnett and Tony Prince would stage a murder in Jensen's flat. Paul

Burnett tells the tale: 'Kid was a fairly naive eighteen-year-old, pretty gullible, I would say. He was doing the late shift and we were all due to meet at his flat for a drink. While we were waiting for him to come home, Noel got a bit bored and said, "Listen, why don't we set this up?" It was quite macabre really, but we thought it was very funny at the time. Noel's idea was that we would pretend he had murdered Tony's wife Christine and then killed himself. Christine would lie on the floor, half under the big double bed. There was to be a liberal amount of tomato ketchup splattered about the place, and David Jensen was to walk in to find Noel had done away with his colleague's missus and stuck his head in a gas oven. It was pretty elaborate: I remember we really pored over details like running a fork through the tomato ketchup to look like scratches. It was hideous really, but it was very funny at the time and, needless to say, we were all pretty tanked up. We'd all been out drinking.

'It had to be timed to perfection. Tony Prince and myself were hidden in the shower; Noel was in the kitchen with his head in the gas oven; and as soon as we heard Kid coming up the stairs, Noel, ever the one to ensure things were as realistic as possible, turned the gas taps on. But it backfired because Kid walked in, saw the scene and, instead of doing what you would expect and turning the gas taps off and pulling Noel's head out of the oven, he dashed off down the street for the police. Tony Prince and I gave chase after him but then, to our horror, realised that Noel was still there with his head in the gas oven, feeling fairly faint by this time. It all ended well but Noel could have actually died! If Kid had made it to the police you can imagine the job we would have had trying to explain all that! But we were young and we did silly things.'

David Jensen remembers finding their 'joke' quite surreal. He says, 'It was about four in the morning in the dead of winter and there was snow on the ground. I'd walked along deserted streets and then through a cemetery in order to get to our apartment, and when I saw the chaos in the house it was mind boggling. They'd really gone to town with ketchup and chip-pan oil all over the floor in the kitchen. They had gone into such detail, most of which I missed, actually. I didn't really take in the finer points, but it was horrible. I ran downstairs to get to a phone. We lived above a bakery and the bakers used to get to work very early, so I thought I could get them to help or I could go across the street to a phone box and call the police. Paul and Tony actually called me from the stairs on the way to the bakery and said, "Kid, Kid, Kid, what are you doing? Where are you going?" Even then I didn't realise it was a practical joke. I asked them, "What are you doing here? What's happening? What's going on?" When they confessed it was all a joke I was just so relieved. I ended up sitting on one of the sofas drinking beer while I watched them do all the cleaning-up.'

Another time, Paul Burnett arrived home to find that all the furniture had been cleared out of his flat. Worse, there was grass growing where the carpets should have been. Even worse, there was a live sheep happily munching away in his living room! No prizes for guessing who was responsible, but – just like when he was at school – Noel called the shots and, surprisingly, never seemed to be on the receiving end himself. 'I don't think we ever played a joke on Noel,' admits Paul Burnett. 'Practical jokes aren't really my scene. I was happy to go along with one of Noel's if it was all good fun and everything, but I'm not one for dreaming them up myself.'

But it wasn't all good times. Noel, like many of the English DJs who were working in Luxembourg, was often homesick. 'Life in Luxembourg is not nearly as glamorous as a lot of people imagine,' he said. 'For a start, the place itself is boring and expensive. Once you've seen the sights there is nothing to do and nowhere to go. And the combination of being in a foreign country and working unsociable hours can easily lead to extreme loneliness. I can remember sometimes crying at night because I felt so lonely. One was particularly vulnerable to this when working the "Dogwatch" – the midnight to 3 a.m. shift. It was a weird feeling to know you were the only person in the building; to lock up when you left and then wander home alone through totally deserted streets.'

Noel hadn't been in Luxembourg long when something happened that gave him a short, sharp shock. After a brief holiday at home in England, Noel had travelled back to Luxembourg in the little Mini Jem kit car which he had built himself with the help of his father. The other DJs had heard endless stories about the car and were looking forward to finally seeing it. Says Paul Burnett, 'We all thought it was quite impressive that Noel had built this thing himself, because he was only nineteen. We were amazed that he had the faith in his own work to do that. But before we even got to see the car Noel was involved in a terrible car crash which you would not have believed anybody could walk away from. The car was split in half – being a kit car it had a fibre-glass body – and a lorry had sliced right through it. Noel was sitting in the front part and the back part was just a total write-off. He is very lucky to be with us today – he got out without so much as a scratch.'

David Jensen also recalls the chaos that day. He was with Paul Burnett at the radio station when the telephone rang with the news of the crash. He says, 'Noel was out and about in this brand-new car when the police telephoned and told us he had been involved in a terrible car accident. We rushed down to the scene – it wasn't too far away from where the radio station was – to find that the car we had been hearing about for months, and had finally come to Luxembourg, had been destroyed. Noel was completely unmarked, which was incredibly lucky because, if you had been walking or driving past the spot, you would have assumed that somebody had died in what was a very messy-looking scene.'

Noel recalled: 'I was sitting at traffic lights when a large lorry ran over the car with me inside it. The driver very kindly stopped when he realised there was no point in attempting to destroy it any more: the Jem was already completely ruined. I crawled out between the front wheels, and was in hospital for about three days with shock. But I did not have a scratch.'

Noel had left England at the height of the swinging sixties, although it would be fair to say he hadn't, at that time, done much swinging himself. One of the disadvantages of being a male only child was that he had a lot of hang-ups about women. 'My mother was my only idea of female company,' he explains. 'I didn't even begin going out with girls until I was eighteen. They seemed to be such a strain that it was easier to stay at home. I thought you had to be polite. I was always waiting for them to go out of the room so I could leap up and open the door for them – I believed it was the mark of a gentleman. And sex before marriage was right out.'

Even compared to Gidea Park, Luxembourg was definitely quiet. It had a population of less than 400,000 and Luxembourgers looked on the British DJs as being strange to say the least. Back home in England, the miniskirt was all the rage. Young women were being encouraged to wear shorter and shorter skirts, with the added incentive of dry cleaners charging two pence per inch for laundering them. Christine Prince explains the culture shock when she and the other trendy young Brits hit Luxembourg. She says: 'Luxembourgers were not like us Brits who had gone over from the swinging sixties. They thought we were strange because a few of the men had long hair and I wore miniskirts. Their way of life was totally different from ours and if we socialised with them they wouldn't come out clubbing with us after. They just didn't do things like that. They were very upper class and set in their ways. They were still in a time warp and their idea of a good time was to hold parties in hunting lodges.'

Compared to London and other cosmopolitan cities,

Luxembourg was several decades behind the times. David Jensen explains: 'It was like life probably used to be during the war. I always had this romantic notion that that was what life was like and Luxembourg probably hadn't changed that much since the 1940s. There was a very small community of English-speaking people in Luxembourg and there was nothing much to do. On Friday nights we used to go to the marines, who used to have a TGI Friday night and nothing much used to happen really. We used to sit around drinking beer and playing pool. Most of the guys from England used to spend all their time wishing they were back there. I remember Noel used to love the idea of going back to England and used to count the minutes and days and hours to when he could be back home.'

Visits to a strip club used to help break the monotony of Luxembourg nights. An early haunt of Noel's and the other DJs was the Club 31 in Hollerich, a suburb of Luxembourg. The club was down by the railway station and it was the only discotheque in Luxembourg. Dave Christian recalls: 'We used to go along and take them free records for the odd free drink and get in for nothing. We used to do about ten or fifteen minutes' jockeying every night. The Club 31 was our place. They had a spiral staircase and a greasy pole which the girls were always asked to slide down. In the days of miniskirts that was a lot of fun!'

David Jensen adds, 'We were working surreal times because our shifts were always very late at night, finishing either at midnight or three or four in the morning, and there were no nightclubs as such. So if you wanted to go on and have a drink with somebody you ended up in a strip club. It wasn't pornographic but it was a strip club none the less.' But while the other, red-blooded young men ogled the sexy strippers, Noel had other, to him at least, more interesting things to occupy his attention. Jensen reveals, 'Noel used to spend a lot of his time in the club dreaming up practical jokes to play on people. He used to sit there writing his ideas down on the back of beer mats.'

Noel's parents visited him in Luxembourg and, says Paul Burnett, were clearly delighted their son was doing so well for himself. 'They were very proud of him and seemed relieved that everything was OK. Noel could have gone to university but he opted for the Radio Luxembourg thing and they were probably very dismayed when he did that, especially when he later got fired. They were probably wondering what the hell was going to happen to him. He is a very bright guy and would no doubt have gone on to do academic things but they seemed pleased that he was happy.'

That Christmas the folks back home in Gidea Park received official Noel Edmonds Radio Luxembourg Christmas cards, sent out by Noel's mother. They were complete with a large black and white photograph of her clean-cut offspring. Wearing a fashionable-yet-inoffensive pullover and slacks and leaning on the bonnet of a white sports car, Noel looked every inch the perfect son. Former-neighbour Janet Coare still has the one sent to her mother Peggy, and recalls, 'Noel's mum was really proud of him. We all got a "Merry Christmas From Noel Edmonds" card that year!' Lydia started a scrapbook of her son's press cuttings while he was at Luxembourg and even to this day Noel says she gets 'terribly upset at any negative stuff'. Noel also did a gig at his father's school – his first as a professional DJ. 'My dad asked me to do a disco in aid of school funds,' he explains. 'But I don't think any of the kids had heard of me.'

Back in Luxembourg, Noel was visited by Chris Fone, who admits to being surprised by how insular life at the radio station was. He explains, 'Noel had no contact with Luxembourgers, so I took him out to clubs – it was very weird because I was the visitor and it should have been him introducing me to the place.

'While I was there I realised that disc jockeys are incredibly insecure. They are very chatty and outgoing on the air but when you meet them in the flesh they are completely different. Generally they were happy to socialise just among themselves.

'Noel was a late developer socially because he had been so very determined and single-minded about becoming successful. I was like his older brother, certainly in wordly terms. He and I discussed the sort of things that maybe much younger boys would discuss.'

During his stay, Chris Fone couldn't help but notice that not everybody was as fond of Noel as he was. He explains, 'There was a certain amount of resentment from some of the other disc jockeys when Noel first arrived, but I'm sure they won't admit to that now. He was inventive and different and that went down very well with the listeners. But it made the other disc jockeys feel insecure. I was aware and sensitive to that and, to a lesser extent, Noel was, too. But he wasn't upset by it. He was far too sure-footed to let it bother him. And then later he became part of the furniture and it was fine.'

Noel enjoyed having his old schoolfriend to stay, not least because it meant he had another target for his practical jokes. Chris says, 'I stayed in his flat and it was great; it was a lot of laughs. He used to do the late slot – and I used to go clubbing while he was on the radio, and we'd meet up again later. But one night he said, "You must come along to the radio station while I'm on the air and see how we go about it." I said, "I can't when you're on the air, don't be daft," but he said, "Of course you can. I am allowed to have guests." I said I wasn't going to be a guest on his programme but in the end I did turn up, with two girls. The girls chickened out and left, so I just sat there drinking coffee while he was on the air. Then he did something terrible to me: he put a piece of paper in front of me with the weather for the United Kingdom. The red light went on and Noel pointed to me and mouthed, "Read the weather." It sounds nothing but he really put me on the spot. He hadn't briefed me or anything so I was there trying to impersonate Noel Edmonds reading the weather. It was just silly boys' games really. The good news was nobody noticed. No one was listening: they were all tucked up fast asleep as it was about four in the morning.'

It was about this time that Noel's colleagues discovered he was a virgin, news that they handled with all the delicacy and tact you would expect from a bunch of guys in their twenties. Dave Christian says, 'One of Noel's girlfriends had come over from England when he first arrived and she was a tweedy-suited person, a schoolteacher type thing. Tony Prince was never backward in coming forward and asked Noel, "Have you fucked it yet?" Noel said, "Oh no, no, we haven't done anything like that," and it casually came out that he hadn't done "it" at all.'

Noel's girlfriend was not seen again. As had happened with the other DJs working in Luxembourg, the distance meant that the relationship simply fizzled out. Christine Prince says, 'Noel wasn't a ladies' man. He was young and I think he was quite shy – he was more into the little car he'd built himself.'

But he came in for endless ribbing once he had revealed the sorry state of his love life to his insensitive colleagues. According to Dave Christian, it was Christine's husband Tony who decided that Noel's virginity was something that must be dispensed with as soon as possible. He recalls, 'Because Noel was still a virgin, Paul Burnett and Tony Prince arranged for him to be "taken care of" by a girl they knew called Elizabeth, who was a stewardess for Air Bahama. It was set up at the Club 31.' But, ever his own man, Noel chose to cling on to his virginity, at least for the time being. Christian continues, 'Needless to say, he didn't go through with it. The rest of the story's good fun because Noel comes out of it a complete prat. Years later when I asked Noel about it he said, "Yes, it's true, but if you ever tell that story I'll sue you." '

Paul Burnett is kinder about Noel's early naivety: 'We had lots of parties and Noel was a typical young male. I don't think he was that experienced when he first came out but he soon made up for lost time.' Tony Prince agrees, saying, 'Noel was just growing up. Puberty had arrived and it was a fantastic time for all of us, particularly for Noel. The girls were queuing up for him. He was very popular. He had come from a very sedate "schoolmarm" background and was suddenly thrust into the wildness of being a DJ for Radio Luxembourg and he made the most of it. He was like a kid in a sweetshop. I suppose that the Radio Luxembourg DJs were the Pied Pipers of the social life – wherever we went people followed us. When the Club 31 closed for the night we'd go to the Chez Nous and sing rock and roll. We had all these stars like Deep Purple and Jimi Hendrix who would come out to be interviewed and then they'd come rocking with us. We were a bit frustrated at living in the centre of Europe but we made the best of it.'

Despite his colleagues' rather unsubtle efforts to 'make a man of him', Noel took his time deciding on the right woman to lose his virginity with. Old-fashioned at heart, Noel wanted to wait until he fell in love. And he wanted to choose the girl himself, not have his mates choose her for him. But, as it turned out, he didn't have to wait long. While he was in Luxembourg he met a beautiful stewardess and fell head over heels for her. Linda Blau was petite, with ash-blonde hair and blue-grey eyes, and was destined to be the first love of his life. She was also the first girl he made love to. Linda worked as a ground stewardess for Loftleider, the airline that later became Iceland Air. It was Chris Fone who was to play matchmaker in Noel's first ever love affair. At a party, Chris, noticing his friend looking miserable and sitting in a corner, asked Linda to go over and see if she could cheer him up. The vivacious blonde immediately worked wonders and before the evening was over Noel was smitten.

Luxembourg, a grand duchy since 1812, was awash with aristocracy and many people had blue-blooded connections, albeit minor ones. Fone recalls, 'She came from a good family and was allegedly a princess. She was the sister of a friend of mine in Luxembourg and she was a very good-looking girl. She was older than Noel, and a great deal more sophisticated. He needed bringing out of himself a bit. He was very shy.'

The young DJ set out to win Linda's heart by romantically dedicating records to her on the radio and taking her out with his DJ friends to the Club 31. Noel told Chris that he felt he'd found 'the right girl', and his colleagues noticed an immediate change in the nineteen-year-old.

Following one of the regular grillings to which Dave Christian and the others subjected the young Noel, he decided it was time to rid himself of the burden of virginity. Dave remembers clearly how Noel singled Linda out to be his first lover: 'It turned out that he and Linda hadn't done "it" either, but one day Noel came into the office with a bottle of champagne and announced that he and Linda were going to go and break it open and do "it" that night.' But, refusing to sink to the rather lewd level of his fellow DJs, Noel kept quiet about the outcome. 'I'm not sure if they did it,' says Christian. 'We never did find out.'

While Christian and the other jocks, in true laddish style, sniggered and made jokes about their young colleague's love life, Chris Fone could see that his light-hearted and impromptu attempt at matchmaking had been successful. Linda was the first girl Noel had really fallen for and, when the relationship ended after only a few short months, Noel was left broken-hearted. It was the first time he had been hurt in that way and he poured out his feelings to his friend in an emotion-packed letter. Fone remembers: 'He was obviously very cut up about it. He had fallen for her in a big way and wasn't prepared for how he would feel when it ended.'

In Luxembourg, Noel also got his first taste of fame and an idea of what was to come as he became an object of hero worship for a whole generation of teenage girls. As Paul Burnett explains, Luxembourg was the ideal place for him to learn how to deal with fame gradually: 'There was a degree of glamour in being a Radio Luxembourg DJ, although our audience was a few hundred miles away back in England. Yes, we were famous but because of the distance involved we didn't have that head-turning effect that fame can have. It can be quite heady stuff. I was about six or seven years older than Noel and the other guys so I was rather a stabilising influence, or so I thought. We always got on very well and I won't say I took him under my wing, but he was always very complimentary about me and felt that I had helped him.'

Although Noel's fans weren't on his doorstep – as they would be once he joined Radio 1 – the fan mail poured in. David Jensen recalls, 'Noel used to keep every single fan letter that was sent to him. He had a drawer full of fan mail. I suppose it was vain, really. He was determined to be famous. I'd never met anyone who had a burning ambition like that before. It was remarkable to see – he was absolutely focused on it.'

Noel hadn't perfected his image in those early days. He was clean-shaven, and those awful multicoloured shirts had yet to make an appearance. David Jensen remarks, 'Noel looked very different then: he was very, very dark. He suddenly went blond when he joined Radio 1.'

But one thing that hasn't changed about Noel over the years is his love of motor racing. Paul Burnett says, 'Noel was always a fan of motor racing and he would talk about that on the air. At one time he even got some dialogue going with a motor magazine back in London. That was quite unusual at the time. Because all the shows were done from Luxembourg, we sometimes felt remote, like we were working in a vacuum. It was great to be able to have some sort of feedback, and Noel was one of the first DJs to bridge that gap.'

Noel made his very first television appearance while he was at Luxembourg – on, of all things, *Come Dancing*. 'A BBC producer heard me on Radio Luxembourg, thought I was a lot older, and booked me to compere the show,' he explains. 'He had a fit when this hairy-bearded youth of nineteen turned up.' He also had to admit that he knew nothing whatsoever about dancing. 'Dancing is a complete gap in my life. I cannot do a step. I was put off at school by a very large lady dancing teacher and have kept away from it ever since.' Nonetheless, Noel holds the unusual honour of being the only person to have hosted *Come Dancing* and *Top of the Pops*.

However, Noel's time on Radio Luxembourg was not a great success. His 'humorous approach' didn't go down well with the station's controller and not even the 'stabilising' influence of Paul Burnett was enough to save Noel from orchestrating his own downfall. After just nine months in the job, Noel's love of pranks was ultimately to result in his being dismissed from the station.

Although Noel initially found life on the station to be new and exciting, the novelty soon began to wear off. The break-up with Linda Blau had also hit him hard and started him thinking about returning to England. A natural entertainer, Noel was always looking at new ways to entertain himself and his colleagues, and, inevitably, this restlessness was to land him in trouble with his bosses.

David Jensen remembers all too well the pointless rules that led to Noel dreaming up ever more outrageous pranks to play on their boss. He says, 'Even though we were working very late at night, we were always required to put in two hours' hanging around the station in the afternoon for absolutely no reason whatsoever. Nobody could ever fathom why we were made to sit there every day doing nothing. Noel used to conjure up tricks to keep us amused because it was so deathly boring.'

Burnett reveals how Noel diced with his job by singling out the head man to be the butt of his pranks: 'There was a guy called John Barter who was supposed to be in charge of us DJs. He wasn't a DJ himself – it was an administrative role – but he took it very seriously. He was something of a little martinet and really got on everybody's nerves. He was a nice enough guy but I think being in charge of some reasonably well-known DJs went to his head. He made our lives a bit miserable, so Noel decided it was time he had his comeuppance.

'It was an old gag but it was still very effective. He taped a large fish to the underside of this guy's knee-hole desk. The smell was just unbelievable and he couldn't trace it to anywhere. People were coming in and they thought it was him. Although it was winter, he had to have all his windows open.'

On that occasion Noel wasn't found out, but his next 'prank' wasn't so subtle. By his own admission, Noel had started to 'muck about' on the air, making his own jingles and telling jokes, and his boss was not amused. Burnett remembers, 'There was a huge double wardrobe in the office, packed full of LPs, and Noel and I put it in front of this guy's office door and then went off to lunch, leaving him quite marooned in there. He was in there for three or four hours and nobody could even hear his cries for help. He was really very precious about it and the upshot of that was that he really had it in for Noel. He turned against him and did everything he could to get Noel removed. At that time Noel was just another DJ – he hadn't been doing it very long – and he was asked to leave. But of course the guy did Noel the greatest favour because after he got the sack he got the Radio 1 job.'

To save face after he was sacked, Noel told his colleagues in Luxembourg that he had been offered a job at Radio 1. This wasn't true, but Noel knew that Radio 1 was where it was *at*, and vowed to become a part of it. He set himself a time limit of four months to get there, after which he would seriously consider university.

But, as it turned out, it was an option that he wouldn't be needing. Radio 1, still in its infancy, viewed Radio Luxembourg as its number-one competitor for the ears of the pop-listening public. For years, Radio Luxembourg had been the perfect talent breeding-ground, and its presenters inevitably ended up working at the BBC. With Radio 1's brief – to get the young, pop-loving, radio-listening public to switch over from Fab 208 to them – they were going to be all too happy to take on the young, and clearly talented, Noel Edmonds.

# 4 The Heady Days of Fame

AFTER THE HUMILIATION of being 'let go' from Radio Luxembourg, Noel picked himself up, dusted himself down and headed to the next port of call on his carefully charted Map to Success: BBC Radio 1. There, in the art deco grandeur of Broadcasting House, he took a poorly paid job making programme trailers with the chance to fill in for the other, more established DJs at weekends.

This latest development in their son's career did not go down well with Mr and Mrs Edmonds. Dudley and Lydia despaired when their son was given the sack. They had wanted him to be a teacher but had supported him when he wanted to take the job at Luxembourg. Now here he was, earning a fraction of what he had been paid at Luxembourg, and little more than a tea boy. It really seemed as if all their son's plans were amounting to nothing.

Noel admits, 'I went from earning £3,500 a year with Luxembourg to £7 a week doing programme trails for the Beeb. But the important thing was that I was working for the BBC – nothing else mattered. The money, or rather the lack of it, didn't bother me that much.'

But Noel was never one to disappoint his parents, and they didn't have to wait long before he was given a break.

His duties involved reading programme trailers and announcing competitions and he was officially required to go in only two days a week. But he spent as much time as he could at Broadcasting House – a place so enormous that he was able to sneak into a small studio on the second floor and spend hours making up his own programmes without being noticed. When he was asked to do a couple of shows in the *Pop Workshop* series – 45-minute programmes that went out during a quiet period on Sunday evenings and were used to test out new DJs – he was able to slip in the sketches and inserts he had come up with during his illicit recording sessions.

He made his first Radio 1 broadcast on 21 July 1969, an historic event slightly overshadowed by Neil Armstrong's walk on the moon, which had happened the day before.

Noel became Radio 1's youngest DJ when he was given his first show, a two-hour programme on Saturday afternoons. Paul Burnett explains how Noel found his niche at the station: 'Noel started working for Radio 1 on a temporary basis doing weekend shows, and very quickly established himself there. In many ways the BBC was an ideal environment for Noel. They gave him his own team of people to work with. He was very creative and he was able to turn his talents to some use there.'

But Noel's big break came when Kenny Everett was sacked by the BBC for a remark he made about the Minister of Transport's wife. Famously off the wall and often outrageous, Everett had already received written warnings from the BBC about his behaviour on the air. As far as his bosses were concerned, it was one joke too many. People in the top echelons of the BBC had wanted Everett's head on a plate and now they had it. Noel was picked to take over Kenny's Saturday show, something he was not entirely happy about. On the one hand it was a fabulous opportunity that was too good to turn down; but on the other hand he liked and admired Everett and was frightened of having to take over from him in such unpleasant circumstances. Would he be ostracised by his fellow DJs? he asked himself. What would the listeners think? What would Kenny think? It was a difficult decision to make.

He recalled: 'Kenny had always been my idol among DJs. He was the guv'nor as far as I was concerned, and by far the greatest influence on my own style. He was a genius. When I read in the paper that he'd got the chop I remember thinking to myself that whoever got the job would find himself in a very difficult position. Trying to follow Kenny would be an unenviable – if not an impossible – task. It didn't cross my mind that I would even be in the running.'

Noel was doing a Radio 1 Club at Weymouth Pavilion – where he had made his debut aged nine – when he was asked to telephone Mark White, the head of Radio 1, and was offered the job. 'This was an enormous break for me, in fact The Break. In career terms, it was like a Fourth Division team's reserve goalkeeper being picked to play for England. I thought to myself, I bet everybody else has gone on strike in protest at the sacking and has refused to do it – I bet I'm the last person they've asked. I asked if I could have time to think about it and was given ten minutes! I then suddenly heard myself saying, "Yes, all right and thank you very much."

'The whole of Fleet Street had been on the phone for me when I got home and at midnight Kenny rang and said, "So, it's you." I told him, "Sorry about that, Ken," but he just said, "Well, best of luck. If you think there is anything I can do, give me a ring. I'll be listening on Saturday. Have fun." It was very touching and was in contrast to DJ Dave Cash, who said to me, "Good luck – you're going to need it." I've always had enormous regard for Dave Cash since then.'

Noel was so excited about taking over from Everett that, on his way home from the studio after his first show, he drove into the car in front and got three penalty points on his licence.

Noel had known that taking over from Kenny would cause resentment, both from listeners and Kenny's friends in the industry. 'For several weeks I found myself under fire from all sides,' he reveals. 'I received letters of frightening abuse from Everett fans who had convinced themselves that I was personally responsible for getting rid of him.'

Everett was a tough act to follow but, if anyone could pull it off, Noel could. And he did. After the first few weeks, when Everett's departure sent the listening figures plummeting alarmingly, they began to creep up again. 'After about nine months they were back to what they had been under Kenny,' said Noel proudly. 'And that gave me enormous personal satisfaction. But for months I was paranoid about Kenny.'

Just when he felt at home in the Saturday slot, Noel was dismayed to be moved to Sunday mornings – an 'off-peak' period. The BBC said they had chosen him in the hope that he would attract more listeners, but Noel was worried he was being demoted. Concerned that his days at the station might be numbered, he vowed to make sure his new show was a hit with the listeners. Helped by his producer, Tim Blackmore, he did just that. 'The work that went into the programme was incredible,' revealed Noel. 'We lived, breathed and ate the show. It was the first occasion on which I'd really built up a rapport with the audience, and I thrived on the quantity and the quality of the mail I received. I was soon enjoying myself so much that when they came along and offered me what was supposed to be the plum promotion – to a daily show – I told them I didn't want to move.'

In June 1973 he was rewarded with the flagship *Breakfast Show*, taking over from Tony Blackburn. The *Breakfast Show* is the most coveted slot in radio for, despite having to get up in the middle of the night to be ready to go on air at 7 a.m., it is the most listened-to show. It was, by anyone's standards, a swift ascent to fame, and even Noel wonderingly remarks, 'It was a meteoric rise. I joined Radio 1 and was suddenly elevated to Tony Blackburn's slot.' If anything, replacing Tony Blackburn was an even more daunting prospect than taking over from Kenny Everett had been. Blackburn had done the *Breakfast Show* since the very beginning of Radio 1. It was Tony Blackburn who had launched the station six years earlier, at 7 a.m. on 30 September 1967, when he cued 'Flowers in the Rain' by

The Move and said, 'Welcome to the exciting new sound of Radio 1.' Back home in Gidea Park, Noel had set his alarm clock to wake him early that day so he wouldn't miss the start of the new station, little guessing that six years later he would be replacing Blackburn himself. Blackburn was enormously popular with listeners, and when Noel took over on 4 June 1973 Blackburn had just been voted top radio disc jockey for the fourth year running. After six years of early starts, he was moving on to the 9 a.m.–noon slot, something he was not happy about.

After running the gauntlet when he took over from Kenny Everett, Noel now had to face the wrath of Tony Blackburn. 'Tony was not at all happy about losing the *Breakfast Show*,' Noel admitted. 'He felt he was being demoted and, to make matters worse, I was the very one he had recognised way back as the young pretender to his throne. I was well aware that he had been looking over his shoulder at me for years, and now he was bound to feel that he had been stabbed in the back. For the first few months our nine o'clock handovers were a little strained.' Matters were probably not helped when Noel couldn't resist having a sly dig at his predecessor: 'The new show will cover a much wider range, still with the occasional LP track, I hope, and a better kind of pop than the music Tony plays,' he said. 'Tony was once quoted as saying that he spoke rubbish on his show. That's the last thing I want to do.'

Tony and Noel were from similar backgrounds and had both been to a private school, yet they were very different. Noel confessed that there were times when the rivalry between him and Blackburn erupted into near violence. He explained: 'We've had our ups and downs. Tony's a complex character but probably his greatest weakness is his insecurity. I first became aware of this when I was at Radio Luxembourg and he gave me a warning lecture about the difficulty of making the grade as a DJ who told jokes. The lecture gradually developed into a blistering attack and that was the first time I realised that he saw me as a threat.

'Much later on, after I had taken over the *Breakfast Show*, we had a titanic row that nearly came to a punch-up and ended with us not speaking to each other for a couple of months. Tony and Tessa Wyatt – who was then his wife – had made a record together under another name and my producer stuck a copy in the box one morning and suggested that I play him a couple of bars at the nine o'clock takeover. I thought he would be delighted and would appreciate a little gee-up with the record – especially as the rules forbade him from playing it on his own show. What I didn't know was that he was convinced that the success of the record depended on keeping the true identity a secret.' Blackburn was livid. 'A tirade of abuse came over the talkback,' said Noel. 'He screamed that I'd wrecked thousands of pounds' worth of work, that this was a top-thirty hit, but now I'd spoilt it by letting out the secret of their identity. It was all very heavy and it went on for a long time. I had to stay in the studio to record another show and he actually went on bad-mouthing me every time he put a record on and came off the air. The engineers loved every minute of it, of course, and it was the talk of the Beeb for days. But I was definitely not amused. I came very near to actually thumping him.'

When he got the *Breakfast Show*, Noel – who was to become the embodiment of mass-appeal radio and television, sneeringly classified as 'lowest common denominator' by highbrow critics – explained his hopes for the programme. His optimistic plan was to lure away Radio 4 listeners, people who were as far removed from the Radio 1 audience as it's possible to be. He said, 'I don't really know yet what sort of audience I will have, but I would like to think that it will expand a bit to include people who are Radio 4 listeners but like a little music as well. So I will include occasional news items and famous quotations. I will remind people of the headlines five years ago, and give them a brain-teaser to think about during the week, still keeping it light, of course. I know the main thing about the early-morning show is the time checks, but I don't feel it's necessary to treat the audience as if they are only semiconscious. I would also like to provoke people a bit. I want to encourage people's minds, not just pump out something designed to sink into the walls.'

Noel's recipe worked. Under him, the *Breakfast Show* achieved record listening figures of 14 million per show, a figure that would be unheard of today. Competition from commercial radio stations has seen Radio 1's listening figures fall from 25 million a week, at its height in the late 1960s, to around 5 million today. But there are those who say that if Noel Edmonds were to go back on the air with a radio show tomorrow he would still attract huge listening figures.

Mike Smith explains Edmonds' unique appeal: 'Noel was aggressively ambitious and I think he probably still is. He was very determined but he also had a talent that really nobody else had at the time, except maybe Kenny Everett. It was a particular talent for communicating with the listener. You can't write about it because you can't describe it, but it was a one-to-one relationship with the listener and there was a certain intelligence about the silliness of the stuff he did on the air. His shows were fantastic.'

Paul Burnett agrees: 'Any radio breakfast show tends to be a mixture of time checks, music and lots of information, but to actually do something that involves the audience listening and paying attention is quite a trick, and Noel is very good at it. He would always get listeners writing in with jokes and anecdotes and I think that's why he did such a good breakfast show at Radio 1.'

On the air, Noel, and his listeners, inhabited a strange make-believe world. He set one of his later shows in an imaginary country house called Dingly Dell. There, Noel and his 'butler', the serious-voiced Radio 4 announcer Brian Perkins, created mayhem in a tiny, fantasy world far removed from the interests and aspirations of the average Radio 1 listener.

Noel's radio style didn't suit everybody, however. Rock

critic Tony Parsons dates the decline of Radio 1 from the day of Edmonds' arrival. 'More than anyone else, he is responsible for turning it into a training ground for game-show hosts,' he said. 'At least Tony Blackburn loved music, but Edmonds didn't. He took Radio 1 from teen to tabloid.'

Noel refutes this: 'I did develop an interest in singer-songwriters like Elton John, but I have never denied the fact that I wasn't a music jock. I always listened more to Kenny Everett than John Peel. But I am actually quite proud of the fact that I developed the concept of personality radio at the BBC. The most satisfying thing for me is when someone says that what I do looks easy. I've always admired people who make things look easy.' Behind the jokes and easy-going banter which Noel employed on air, there was a deadly seriousness. He revealed how he enjoyed getting stressed before going on air, something he still does today with *House Party*. 'I prefer to be tense at the beginning of a show,' he said. 'Otherwise I make silly mistakes.'

For Noel, one of the saddest things about departing Radio Luxembourg had been leaving behind the good friends he'd made there. David Jensen would eventually end up at Radio 1, as did Paul Burnett. Burnett stayed at Radio Luxembourg for another five years after Noel left, but the friendship he and Noel formed in Luxembourg was not forgotten. Generous-natured, Noel later used his influence at the BBC to help Burnett land a job at Radio 1. Burnett says, 'I joined Radio 1 in 1974 and I probably have Noel to thank for that. I came over when I was still at Radio Luxembourg and I was invited to go to one of the Brands Hatch days out, which was a Radio 1 thing. I didn't realise it at the time, but I was being sounded out for a job and a few months later I was part of it. I later realised the day had been almost like an audition and it had been Noel's doing.'

Working at Radio 1 was like being part of a huge extended family, an experience only-child Noel found both novel and fun. In 1972, Johnny Beerling, executive producer of Radio 1, launched the Radio 1 Roadshow, the annual summer tour around Britain's seaside resorts. Prior to the Roadshows, the disc jockeys would enjoy 'weeks away': glorious, carefree weeks that were supposed to be about work but which inevitably ended up as one long laugh. Paul Burnett remembers: 'We used to have weeks away up and down the country, usually to coincide with the launch of a new local radio station. We would descend on the town and we'd all stay in a hotel for a week, kicking off with a charity football match or something like that. It was great fun because we would get to know each other terribly well – male bonding we'd call it now.'

Noel found himself to be a willing player in these 'male-bonding' sessions, not least because they presented him with the perfect opportunity for playing practical jokes. In this he was in fine company. Fellow Radio 1 DJ Mike Read was an infamous perpetrator of practical jokes and, until the arrival of Noel, had been principal prankster at the station. During their frequent weeks away in dull provincial towns, the disc jockeys, fuelled by boredom and alcohol, gave their imagination free reign as they dreamt up ever more elaborate jokes and scams. The more complex and involved they became, the more Noel liked them. Noel's pranks, like the ones he'd played on Paul Burnett and David Jensen in Luxembourg, were sophisticated and detailed. Not so Mike Read's 'jokes'. Paul Burnett explains: 'It was rather childish, I know, but on one occasion, when we were staying at a hotel in Leeds, Mike brought along a load of stink bombs which he placed under people's lavatory seats. They would sit on the lavatory seat and there would be this really awful smell. It was February and your room would be totally unlivable because you had to have all your windows open in the freezing cold.

'He'd done it to Noel; he'd done it to everybody; and it was decided it was time he got his comeuppance. I remember it was fairly elaborate and we planned it like a military offensive. We met in Noel's room and we all put in our tuppence worth and generally ended up with a good

Gotcha. The general scenario was that Mike would go into his hotel room, sit on the bed – which would collapse because the legs had been removed and it was just resting on little pegs. He would then go to the bathroom and the door would fall off in his hands because the hinges had been removed, and there would be some live chickens in the bath which Dave Lee Travis had supplied from his farm. The whole effect was pretty dramatic to say the least. There were a couple of other things – it was kind of a domino effect. But again, as is often the case with these things, it kind of backfired.

'We had told the hotel what we were going to do and the staff were very good about it and let us have the room next door to his so we could hear what was going on. We were waiting for Mike to go to his room but when he did he had a young lady on his arm. Mike had had a few drinks and we heard them go into his bedroom. They sat on the bed, which promptly collapsed – she laughed at that. But she then went to the bathroom: the bathroom door fell in, chickens flew everywhere in a panic all over the room, and that was it – she'd had enough. She ran out screaming. I don't know what she must have thought, poor girl. She left Mike there muttering to himself. He couldn't understand what the hell was going on. We ruined his night of lust. The last we heard he was talking rather amorously to one of the chickens! We put the room back as it was but whether the chickens ever recovered I don't know! But if you give it out you've got to take it and, to give him his due, Mike did take it very well. I think the seeds for Noel's TV Gotchas were sown then. In fact, Noel told me once that the Hit Squad idea came from there.'

The year 1970 was a momentous one for Noel. Not only had he landed his own show at Radio 1, putting the seal of success on the radio career that he had begun two years before, but he also fell in love with the woman who was to become his first wife. Noel's painful split from air stewardess Linda Blau back in Luxembourg had left him feeling cautious and wary of getting his heart broken for a second time. Nineteen-year-old Gillian Slater was the first girl he had met since Linda whom he felt he could take that risk with. They met in May 1970 at a party at the London Hospital in Whitechapel, where Gill was studying to be a physiotherapist. To start with she did not believe anything he told her about what he did for a living. She thought it was all a big wind-up until she heard him on the radio a few days later. Noel, never the smoothie, recalls his cringing chat-up line: 'She was wearing something that looked like a tablecloth,' he says. 'So I walked over and said, "You've got my mum's tablecloth on!" The following Saturday I played a record for her on my show. She was driving her father's car at the time and when she heard her name she drove straight into a ditch.'

The morning after he met Gill, a lookalike of Ali McGraw, the star of the 1970s film *Love Story*, Noel told an interviewer, 'I fell in love last night with a physiotherapist. Lovely she is. But I'll probably fall in love with someone else next week. That's what youth is for, isn't it?' But Noel didn't fall in love with anyone else. The more he saw of Gill, the more he liked her. In many ways Gill was the perfect girl for him. She was a pretty, nice, middle-class young woman from a similar background to his, and, significantly, had nothing to do with the shallow world of show business. She was the daughter of a chartered accountant and still lived at home with her parents in Shenfield, Essex. And because they had met so early in his career, Noel could be sure that it was him she liked, not the trappings of his fame. He said, 'With Gill I knew it was me she fell in love with because when we met and married I had nothing.'

Chris Fone remembers the early days of Noel's courtship of Gill: 'Noel met Gill not long after he came back to England. In Luxembourg you could say that he didn't really know much about girls but he started to learn. Then, when he came back to his roots, he was far more outgoing and started to socialise more. The social scene at that time revolved around a particular pub near Shenfield, called The Rose. Noel started going there as one of the boys, for the first time in his life probably. Before he went to Luxembourg he never socialised in that way because he was too busy concentrating on becoming successful.

'Gill was very nice, a very strong personality. She certainly was the sort of girl who was exceedingly popular with all the boys, but I don't mean that in a tarty way. She was super company; she was the life and soul of the party; and Noel needed that to bring him out of himself. I wasn't surprised when he told me he wanted to marry her. I think Noel had a need and she obviously met it. I think he needed to get away from an overdominant mother and make his own way in the world. I very much got the impression that Noel got married because he felt it was time to get married; it was all part of his grand plan.'

Noel got on well with Gill's parents. Initially horrified that their precious daughter was dating a disc jockey, Geoffrey and Margaret Slater were quickly won over by Noel's easy charm, and not a little relieved to see a nice middle-class young man where they had imagined an oik. Geoffrey, now retired, vividly recalls his first meeting with his future son-in-law: 'We were living in Shenfield when Gillian brought him home one day. When we had first heard that our daughter was pairing up with a disc jockey, as they were then called, I was horrified. Disc jockeys were not really a parent's idea of the perfect man, and I thought, Yuk! But when we met him we were quite favourably impressed. It turned out he lived at Gidea Park with his parents, which was very close to us. We knew Gidea Park because we had lived there ourselves. He was a different being from what I imagined disc jockeys were. He was much more intelligent. He'd had a good schooling and had done reasonably well at school. He was an intelligent disc jockey as distinct from a zombie, so we were very impressed. We met him several times after that and we liked him. We got on extremely well.'

When Noel decided he wanted to make Gill his wife, the traditional side of him wanted to do things right and ask her parents' permission. But, true to form, Noel, never one to do things normally, came up with a novel way of asking Geoffrey for Gill's hand in marriage. A six-foot-by-four-foot crate appeared on the Slaters' doorstep one morning, containing a very small object. Geoffrey explains, 'Noel had a record made. It was a little ten-inch record done in a recording studio with a group to do the background music. He did a little thing about wanting to marry my daughter. He didn't actually sing it: he spoke the words. We sat and listened to this, which amused us, and I said, "Yes, of course." '

Noel and Gill became engaged on 17 November 1970, a doubly special day, for it was also Gill's 21st birthday. At their engagement party in Mayfair, Noel said, 'I don't believe in love at first sight, but it was pretty close.' To celebrate his engagement he bought a Rover 2000 to add to his collection of four cars. He said, 'Apart from the engagement ring, I haven't bought Gill anything yet.' And added with a wink, 'Anyway, she thinks I am the best present she has ever had.' Gill replied, 'He's right, even if it is a bit big-headed of him to say so himself.' Noel also announced that he wouldn't be living with his fiancée until they were married. 'I'm square in some ways compared with some of my disc jockey colleagues,' he said. 'I want to get married in the old-fashioned way.'

Other DJs' wives offered advice to Noel's fiancée. 'Build up your sense of humour,' said Terry Wogan's wife Helen. 'Otherwise you will burn with frustration at parties when everybody wants to talk to your man, while you stay in the background.' And Dave Cash's wife Dawn warned the young couple about the problem of loneliness. She said, 'DJs have to travel a lot, so you can't make long-term social plans – ask people to dinner and so on. If you do, as sure as fate, he'll be whisked off somewhere.' Steamily erotic letters from fans shouldn't matter, she said. 'There's no point in being jealous because that is all part of your husband's work. And if he tells you he is working late you need never wonder if it's only an alibi. You can check by turning on the radio.'

The wedding was duly arranged and took place the following year, on 10 July 1971 at Gill's parents' local church, St Mary's in Shenfield. Geoffrey was one of the couple's witnesses; Noel's father Dudley was the other. The reception was held at the Masonic Hall. Geoffrey Slater remembers, 'Noel invited several of his BBC friends. Mickey Most was there and some other people we didn't know.'

The newlyweds settled down to married life in a small first-floor flat in New Ash Green, Kent. Then, when Noel took over the *Breakfast Show* two years later, they needed to find somewhere closer to London, so Noel paid £25,000 for a run-down three-bedroomed semi in Hampstead Garden Suburb. At that time Noel saw a lot of Paul Burnett. Burnett explains, 'When we were both at Radio 1 in the 1970s we used to socialise quite a lot. He and Gill were a young married couple and they had a little place in Hampstead which they'd done up themselves, all the usual things young married couples do. I think Noel was reasonably well known when they met, but not telly famous, which is where real fame is. She was nice: we all liked Gill. And I must say that, unlike some of the other well-known people I have worked with, Noel wasn't insular then. He liked parties. He liked holding them and he liked coming to them. Gill was sociable, but rather shy, and I would have thought it was Noel rather than her who was the moving force behind the dinner parties and the socialising.'

Noel remained close to his parents and he and Gill would often spend weekends back in Gidea Park, where the superstar's visits home caused a stir among the neighbours. Julie Howie, who lived next door to Noel's parents in Risebridge Road, recalls, 'Noel had already moved out when we bought our house and I didn't know that we were living next door to his mum and dad for about a fortnight – until we went for a stroll one evening. His mother used to have a big photograph of him in the window, facing outward. They were very proud of him and they talked about him a lot and showed me pictures of him. They had photograph albums of his press cuttings and they used to lend them to me to look at.'

A lot of time was spent with Gill's parents, with whom they holidayed in the Lake District. Geoffrey Slater liked Noel enormously and considered him a friend as well as a son-in-law. The two would often go out together for a companionable drink at the local pub. Noel would share the details of his many weekends in Shenfield with his listeners. Geoffrey Slater explains, 'We had quite a big garden in those days and when they came to stay we would sometimes play badminton. The next morning on Radio 1, Noel would start the programme by saying, "I spent the weekend with Lord and Lady Fairmead." Fairmead was the name of our house in Shenfield. He'd say, "I played badminton on the top lawn and ate cucumber sandwiches," all of which was a load of codswallop!'

At that time in his life it seemed to Noel that everything was really coming together. He was enjoying Radio 1 and was a happy young newlywed. But, never one to rest on his laurels, he realised that DJ-ing was not just about having fun on the air. The business acumen that he had developed as a schoolboy spurred him on and encouraged him to make the most of every opportunity. Even in the early days at Radio 1, Noel marketed his image astutely, leaving his studio in the morning to open supermarkets in the provinces, or else spending the afternoons in the studios of Wardour Street, recording commercial voice-overs for soap powder.

One such voice-over made headlines in March 1973 when he featured in the first radio commercial for contraceptives. But the advert, which was, ironically, aired on Radio Luxembourg, almost didn't get made, for two reasons. First, Luxembourg laws prohibited 'the import, manufacture and transport and distribution of contraceptives' and banned publicity for them. Secondly, Noel turned down the first script by Durex for being too personal. 'They wanted to use my wife's name in it, which we didn't want,' he said. 'Apart from that it identified us too closely with the product. It looked as if it was the particular type and brand of contraceptive we preferred.'

In fact, Gill, he revealed, was on the pill. Children did not figure in their plans. 'I can't imagine us having children,' he said at the time. 'Not at the moment anyhow – that would be disastrous. The idea of being woken up at three in the morning when I have to get up at a quarter to five just doesn't appeal. I'll wait until some brilliant obstetrician invents a way of babies being born at five years old without making the lady's eyes water too much!'

During his early years at Radio 1, Noel became close friends with Mike Smith, and the two forged a bond that was to prove to be one of the most important and significant relationships in both their lives. Mike, speaking for the first time about the depth of their friendship, recalls how he met Noel in 1973 when he was an eighteen-year-old schoolboy and Noel was just about to take over the Radio 1 *Breakfast Show*. He says, 'I first met him at Brands Hatch at one of those weird event things he used to do, called the Disc Jockeys' Race. I was there racing my own car that day and I read in the programme notes at the meeting that Noel wanted to do some more proper racing. So I tracked him down that afternoon and introduced myself. I said, "Well, I've heard you on the radio but you don't know who the hell I am. Would you like to do some racing in my car?"

'He said he would but unfortunately the very first time he got in the driver's seat he wrote the car off. It wasn't even the proper race: he destroyed it in practice. He went off the track and crashed it. He was OK, which of course was the most important thing, but the car was completely trashed and to someone who was eighteen years old it was very valuable. It was everything I had and he destroyed it. He was very concerned about that. He didn't offer any money, which was a portent of things to come, but he stayed in touch and was very concerned that I got the car rebuilt and got back racing again.

'We forged a curious friendship. I was quite in awe of him. I really loved his style on the radio. I thought he was fantastic. And we were both Essex boys: he came from Gidea Park and I was born about three or four miles away. I looked upon Noel as an older brother. He was very much an only child and I think he quite liked having me around, almost as a kid brother. There is a seven-year age difference between us and I was still at school when he was doing his stuff. Noel started very early and he climbed very quickly.'

It was Mike's admiration of Noel which inspired him to follow in his footsteps and seek a career in radio. He explains, 'At the time, I listened to the radio but I wasn't interested in broadcasting – I wanted to be an actor. But Noel occasionally used to invite me up to Radio 1 to watch him on the *Breakfast Show* and, once I had seen him work, I thought, I want to do that. I realised it was a far more lucrative profession than acting and that Noel was having a lot more fun than I would ever have had in the theatre. So I said to him, "Look, you could help me out a bit here, I really quite fancy doing what you're doing." '

Showing the same generosity of spirit that he had shown Paul Burnett, Noel was only too happy to oblige. He willingly used his influence at Radio 1 to put in a good word for his young protégé. Mike says, 'It was Noel who got me my first job. I had worked behind the scenes with him at Radio 1 and after a while he introduced me to Johnny Beerling, who was the executive producer at Radio 1. Johnny said, "Look, we don't give jobs to inexperienced people but why don't you come and make some programme trailers for us?" And so, in about May 1975, I went and worked at Radio 1 once a fortnight. I would get £12 to go in and make programme trailers, some of which were for Noel's shows. The rest of the time I was trying to make ends meet. I was still living at home; my father was dying; and I was working all over the place trying to get myself on to my feet.'

At this time in the mid-1970s, Noel was one of the most well-known people in the country and had an enviable lifestyle. Put bluntly, he was making a packet. The Radio 1 DJs were every bit as famous as the pop stars whose records they played, and Radio 1 was dubbed 'Radio Gold Dust', referring to the lucrative personal appearances which earned the DJs a small fortune. Noel's basic salary for doing the *Breakfast Show* was £10,000 a year, but he could make a tenth of that for just one night's work at a disco. During one nine-month period, Noel travelled 35,000 miles from gig to gig. 'In one week I went to Devon on the Monday and then back home; to Sunderland for Tuesday night; then south to London to record *Top of the Pops*. On Thursday I was back up North again in Newcastle, and on Friday I headed back to Devon, with a journey home each time,' he said. 'It was totally mad. I found I was driving regularly at ninety miles an hour on the motorways. This was because we had a gadget that plugged into the cigar lighter to brew the tea and unless we were going fast the water didn't boil. If I had been stopped for speeding at least I could have offered the police a hot cup of tea.'

Noel made his first *Top of the Pops* appearance in 1972, and throughout the 1970s he was one of the most frequent presenters of the weekly show, and one of the most popular. He says of his first show, 'I thought I was fantastic but my wife said I looked like a Madame Tussaud's reject which had been taught to talk. When I saw a recording I could see I was shaking like a leaf.' *Top of the Pops* was an important stage in Noel's career as it provided a perfect opportunity for him to get used to being in front of the camera. It also brought him to the attention of a whole new audience and gave him a sky-high earning potential.

While other radio jocks basked in the reflected glamour of rock, Noel was dazzled by the allure of business. He swiftly realised there was money to be made out of sponsorship and advertising, and set about marketing himself as a product. 'I sell myself,' he said bluntly. 'Basically my job is the promotion of my personality and various parts of my body.'

Mike Smith recalls how Gill was the power behind the throne as far as Noel's finances were concerned: 'She was the one who clued him in to running himself as a business. He does all his own negotiations and he's never needed to have much of a manager because all of his TV work is with the BBC. He does one contract negotiation every four years and that's it, and he has always had an office through which things can be referred.'

Noel realised what an asset he had in Gill. She had her feet firmly on the ground and wasn't the type to come over all giddy when his fame and wealth started to grow. She had qualified as a physiotherapist but never practised, preferring to devote her time to looking after Noel: Noel the business as well as Noel the husband. It didn't make sense to pay for a secretary, she reasoned, when she could do the job twice as well herself. She answered his fan mail by hand from the office Noel set up for her in a corner of their home. Little did the besotted women who wrote to him know that the object of their affections would sit in bed reading their letters with his wife. She drove him upward of a thousand miles a week around Britain so he could make his lucrative personal appearances, and she negotiated his fees and dealt with his business contacts.

Because he had time to do only one in five of the things he was offered, most of the time Gill dispensed with the preliminaries and got down to the nitty gritty of quoting his basic charge. 'His fee for spending an hour at a club in the evening is £250, take it or leave it,' she said in 1974, the same year that Noel said he could easily take his earnings up to £100,000 if he wanted to. 'People who are really established charge much more,' she added. 'Of course, if a club wanted to tie Noel up exclusively for a year it would cost thousands and thousands. Noel is working hard while the going is good. He is getting up at 5 a.m. and does the show from seven to nine. Then there are lots of other things, like doing voice-overs for commercials, launching things and opening places, and a small amount of modelling. One way and another we travel about a thousand miles a week. We have got a part share in a record shop in the King's Road, too.'

Unlike many of the trophy wives who clung to the arms of other celebrities, Gill was more interested in helping her husband make money than she was in spending it: 'We have to be realistic. This isn't going to last for ever, so I don't go on enormous spending sprees. We go on expensive holidays, like to Jamaica last year and the Seychelles this year, but we are not really extravagant. Noel likes a good car because he is keen on racing, but our other extravagance is really an investment – a cottage in Norfolk. It is three hundred and fifty years old, with three attic bedrooms, completely unspoilt, with beams and uneven walls. It is nice having plenty of money but I don't think of us as being rich because one has to think of the future. DJs don't last for ever.'

Gill, daughter of an accountant, inevitably had a respect for money. Words like 'sensible', 'investment' and 'realistic' were what mattered in life. 'Extravagant' and 'spending sprees' were words to feel ashamed about. In this, she was ideally suited to Noel. He shared her high regard for money and he didn't need to worry that she would squander away his hard-earned cash on clothes and jewellery like other wives of famous men might do. Noel congratulated himself on choosing such a clever wife. He said in an interview, 'I'm discovering what a remarkable girl I have married. She accepts me as I am, but she's really rather special, adapting herself to so many different lifestyles. She's a girl in a million and I wouldn't swop her for anyone else in the world.' Gill even did his worrying for him: 'Marriage has brought me a full-time, unpaid professional worrier – my wife Gilly. She loves getting upset so she does the worrying for both of us while I stay cool, calm and dynamic.'

And she shared his love of cars, loyally supported his interest in motor racing and even acted as his codriver in the Tour of Britain Rally in 1974. They both ended up in hospital when their Ford Escort came off the road, overturned and landed in a ditch. Gill's crash helmet split open and Noel later realised that one more roll might have smashed her skull. Noel was in a worse state: he couldn't move and doctors were worried he had broken his back. He had an agonising five-hour wait before specialists gave him the all-clear.

Noel willingly admits that he got a kick out of living dangerously. Driving a souped-up car at breakneck speeds gave him a rush unlike anything he had ever experienced. 'I treasure that lovely moment when I've got away with something that's quite incredible. I get a tingling sensation on the spine. It's like nothing else in the world,' he said. 'Although my own death doesn't frighten me, I worry about what it would do to my parents. If I were quite truthful I'd say some of these activities were really selfish on my part, but I can't help myself. I want to experience fear so as to enjoy it, control it and learn more about myself. I don't see why fear should always be distasteful. Too many of us think of it as something to avoid, like sadness or depression.'

During his time on the *Breakfast Show*, Gill would go up to bed with him even if she wasn't feeling tired 'because he doesn't like to go to bed by himself'. It seemed the only thing that Gill Edmonds didn't do for her husband was find him funny. But even this she blamed on herself: 'I simply don't find Noel funny,' she said. 'I think a lot of his jokes are silly, but then I haven't got much of a sense of humour. The only time I ever laughed at him was when he tripped over a cement bucket when the decorators were replastering the sitting room.'

In 1974, Noel was offered seven racing sponsorships after winning two disc jockey races at Brands Hatch the year before, and he insured himself for £50,000. As his fame grew and the offers continued to flood in, it became clear that Gill couldn't cope with everything herself. Noel was always reluctant to give an outsider control in his life and is unique among his show-business colleagues in never having had a manager. But over the years he has enlisted the services of various professionals: promotions specialists, personal assistants and advisers. It was at this stage in his career that Noel met promotions executive Derek James. Their business relationship endured for more than ten years and for a while the two were friends.

But, James reveals, their relationship floundered almost before it had even begun: 'I first met him when he was doing his afternoon show on Radio 1. I booked him to do a personal appearance at a nightclub but we ended up falling out in quite a big way over money. It was just a silly thing but fame had gone to his head quite a bit because he'd just been offered the *Breakfast Show*. The contract said cash on the night, which was a regular contract of ours, but at this particular venue all the tills had been cashed up by the time Noel was ready to go and the guy said he would have to accept a cheque. 'I gave Noel the cheque and he threw a complete wobbly and said, "When the contract says cash, it means cash." And I said, "Noel, I'm telling you now that if there's any trouble with that cheque I will cover it." But he just stomped off and roared out of the car park.'

Not long after that, Noel was forced to cut down on the volume of personal appearances he was doing after he blacked out and collapsed on stage just minutes after finishing a broadcast from a Derby youth club. It gave him an enormous shock because, at 24, he should have been in excellent health. The doctor diagnosed overwork and Noel had to face facts and reduce his workload. 'Of course, everybody assumed I was drunk – I was aware of the whispers as they carried me back to the dressing room,' he said ruefully. 'I had been going through a particularly hectic patch and I was totally washed out. There was a time when I couldn't say no to anything. Anyone who rang asking me to open fêtes, compere shows, present prizes – you name it and I would agree. It was a kind of panicky thing. I thought if I said no I wouldn't get asked to do anything more. I sat down one night and thought, This has got to stop.'

But instead of standing by and watching his income drop, Noel cannily decided to do less work for the same amount of money. 'I decided to price myself out of some of the business, and doubled my fee when offered discotheque gigs.' Even Noel was amazed when his audacious plan worked. 'It was amazing! The promoters were taken aback, but all of them rang back in the end and said, "Right, you're on." It has become like roulette – they think they'll get me if they offer more and more money.' Noel was making so much money that way back in 1973 he said, 'If I gave up work tomorrow, I think I could get by financially for the rest of my life.'

If the Radio 1 DJs were treated like national pop stars, just like the members of top rock groups, they were also subject to considerable attention from 'jockeys', the DJ's equivalent to groupies. 'I'm amazed at the things women will confess to someone who is just a voice on the radio,' he said. 'It is noticeable from my mail that women love to talk about anything to do with sex.' And some of them wanted to do more than just talk about it. 'Girls write to me suggesting all sorts of things,' Noel confessed in an early interview. 'There's a woman in Ipswich who sends me photographs, and another woman, Mary from Cleethorpes, wrote, "Dear Noel, I've seen you on *Top of the Pops*, and I wish to make the scene with you. I know you are married, but I am engaged, so that is all right. I will come to London and we can meet. I am very discreet. I never mention names." That is my favourite letter. I am buying a very expensive frame and putting it up on the wall. I did think of inviting Mary to an office at the studio, getting her to take off all her gear and then telling the producer someone wanted to see him. But it seemed a bit mean really.

'There is always a group of girls outside discos, of course, and it's very clear what their idea is. You would have to be out of your mind to do anything about it. There was this drunk girl in Aberdeen who asked me to autograph her arm and I said flippantly, "What, only your arm?" She kept after me then and eventually, I suppose to cover my embarrassment, I told her my room number at the hotel. It was the wrong number, mind you, but the right hotel. When I got back that night I found her lying asleep on the floor outside someone else's room. I left her there – and I don't make flippant comments to girl fans any more.'

Groupies were an occupational hazard. They took to hanging around wherever Noel was, whether it be outside Radio 1, the *Top of the Pops* studio, or even his own home. Occasionally, Noel and Gill would take refuge at the Somerset home of Chris Fone and his wife Sue. Chris explains, 'Noel and Gill used to come and visit us when they were down this way. We were a safe house where the little girls weren't screaming. Mind you, he didn't help with his very ostentatious motor cars, and his personalised number plates before they were commonplace. He enjoyed the limelight.'

In 1975, Noel received his Disc Jockey of the Year Award from Princess Anne. In the mobile souvenir shop that travelled with the Radio 1 Roadshow around Britain's coastal resorts that summer, 25p posters of Noel hung next to posters of Slade, Paul McCartney and Elton John. Girls scrawled sexy messages to Noel on their bras and panties, which they would fling at his feet when he was on stage. There was an unpleasant side to his fame as, just like Helen Wogan had warned, fans ignored Gill and wanted to talk only to her husband. Worse, she had obscenities shouted at her by girls jealous that she was married to Noel. She said, 'Occasionally when he opens school fêtes, he gets mobbed and people climb on the stage and start tearing at his clothes – I find that a bit frightening.' Initially amused by the fantasy world some of his fans inhabited, she said, 'I think they believe that after a show Noel and I go off to some fairy-tale mansion instead of going home to cut the grass. They say to me, "Oooh, it must be wonderful to live with him." I tell them, "You don't have to wash his underpants." '

Even Noel got fed up with it on occasions. 'Many people have the wrong impression about this work,' he said. 'It's not that easy. It interferes with your private life. Imagine waking up and finding girls camped on your front lawn, and having to ring the police to take them away. And when we're out, people almost walk straight through my wife to get to me. That is not nice for any wife.'

As well as having to come to terms with the adulation that accompanied his fame, Noel found it hard adjusting to the early mornings that the *Breakfast Show* required. He reveals, 'I had a problem when I first started the *Breakfast Show*. You have to get out of bed and be bang on form, which means you have to be completely disciplined. But my time clock went out of gear and I was coming home at 10 a.m. and having a couple of gin and tonics. Then one week I noticed that I had put away two bottles and I thought, Christ, this is serious, so I cut back.' And he readily agreed when asked whether there was a certain selfishness behind a life so meticulously organised. 'Selfish? Yes, I think I am. But then, isn't everybody? I mean, it's number one for survival, isn't it?'

As Noel's fame grew, those close to him began to feel uncomfortable with the effect it was having on him. Chris Fone, his friend for more than twenty years, explains how Noel changed under the spotlight of megastardom. He says, 'I had mixed emotions about Noel's success. In one way I was quite pleased for him when he decided to get a different kind of life for himself, but I wouldn't have chosen the company he ended up tending to keep. In a funny way, Noel was quite an innocent person. It may sound odd, and I'm sure he wouldn't see it that way, but he was very naive and innocent then. He had always chosen to be his own man and had been very particular in the company he kept. But later on, during his years at Radio 1, he wasn't very discerning. I found it all a bit false.

'At that time it was very wearing if you were a friend of Noel's because you tended to be carted around. He was terribly generous with his money and would drag me off here, there and everywhere, to Brands Hatch and other big events, but in a way I felt I was being shown off to. Noel just couldn't see that these people were using the glitz for their own ends. It wasn't him I objected to; it was just the company he was keeping. I thought he was demeaning himself, which he was.'

Gill also saw the change in her husband and did not like what she saw. Noel's father-in-law had noticed how different Noel had become as well. He remarks, 'Fame went to his head and he got a bit too big for his boots. From then on it got very, very complicated and all a bit silly really. It ended up that we didn't get on and because of that we hardly saw our daughter. It was a very, very difficult time.'

Noel was beginning to realise what a powerful aphrodisiac fame can be, and was setting out on a dangerous path that would eventually lead him to the divorce courts. But his close friends believe that, at that particular stage in his life, Noel was blinded to the risks he was taking. There was no reasoning with him. In any case, he had other things on his mind.

He had set his sights on a move into television, an expansion he felt was necessary to his career. In 1973, Noel had been dismissive of the allure of the small screen, saying, 'Television sucks you up, chews out all your talent, then spits you away like a drawn grape. At least radio offers some sort of stability. It is my particular medium, I'm sure.' But three years later he had come to change his mind. Always inventive, Noel was keen to try different things and was beginning to feel the restrictions of radio.

Now he was ready to take it one step further. In 1976, he was poised on the brink of a whole new chapter in his life, a career change that would eventually make him a millionaire and, ultimately, one of the most powerful men in broadcasting. But heartache was also just around the corner, and his personal life was about to be torn apart.

# 5 Lights, Camera, Action!

NOEL WORKED HARD at forging a career for himself in television, displaying the same energy and determination that had taken him to the top of his tree in radio. He was no longer satisfied with being 'Noel Edmonds the DJ'. He now wanted a name so famous it would need no job description tagged on the end. 'I have always wanted to establish "Noel Edmonds" as a name everybody would know,' he admitted.

He knew he was facing an uphill struggle. Noel said, 'The history of disc jockeys getting into television and being seriously accepted is very poor indeed. There is still a sort of stigma attached to being a DJ. It somehow ranks alongside second-hand-car salesman and glamour photographer as one of those jobs that doesn't quite sound *right*. Any reasonably ambitious person – and I'm *very* ambitious – wants to establish himself as an individual. I can remember the tremendous thrill the first time an article called me "Noel Edmonds, Radio 1 disc jockey". But it is an even greater thrill if I am now called simply "Noel Edmonds".'

The children's Saturday-morning show *The Multicoloured Swap Shop* went a good way to achieving this for Noel. As one of Radio 1's most popular disc jockeys, he was already a household name, but television brought him a whole new legion of fans and propelled him into a different league altogether. As he remarked at the time, 'I reckon I must be among the ten most-recognised people in the country.'

But he almost hadn't taken the job because he already had

a gruelling workload. He was still making his usual frequent appearances hosting *Top of the Pops*, as well as appearing on television on the panel of *New Faces*. In 1976, he was offered the chance to expand his television experience by presenting *Illusionists*, a six-week BBC magic show, and he also made his acting debut in the BBC2 play *Glitter*, in which he played – a disc jockey and *Top of the Pops* presenter called Noel Edmonds. He had dabbled in children's television for the first time the year before with *Z-Shed*, an after-school agony phone-in programme. It was not a success, but Noel's second attempt at children's TV was to be an immediate hit.

He agreed to do *Swap Shop* because he had a feeling that 'it was something special, something not be be missed'. The show was launched on 2 October 1976 in direct opposition to London Weekend Television's *Lively Scene*, presented by Sally James. It was a replacement for the usual Saturday-morning run of cartoons and dubbed French shows like *Belle and Sebastian* and *Robinson Crusoe*. During the three-hour show, children were encouraged to ring in and ask celebrity guests questions and voice their opinion on things. There was also a swap shop where children could exchange items by phone. Kids would ring in offering to exchange back copies of comics and football magazines for other desirable items. 'We will swap anything so long as it's not alive,' said Monica Sims, the Head of Children's Entertainment at the BBC. 'Not your brother for a sister, or your budgie for a vulture, but we're ready to try to fix an exchange for anything you've got, providing it's not broken.'

When *Swap Shop* began, the BBC crossed their fingers and hoped for an audience of 4 million. They got twice that. It trumped the opposition and became one of the biggest successes in the history of BBC Television. Initially scheduled to run for thirteen weeks, it ended up running for six years. Its fresh format was followed by kids programmes such as *Saturday Superstore*, *Going Live!* and *Live and Kicking*. LWT tried to dent the show's success by launching

*Tiswas* with Sally James and the then unknown Chris Tarrant, but *Swap Shop* reigned supreme.

Noel, who became known to millions of kids as 'The *Swap Shop* Man', recalls: 'Back then, the BBC didn't start broadcasting until around 9.30 a.m. on Saturday mornings, and then all they showed was old movies and *The Flashing Blade*. *Swap Shop* was a real departure. All I had was a running order; there wasn't much script. We used to get the crew to join in – it's common now but back then it was radical stuff. I remember one of our technicians was disciplined because he forgot where he was and laughed out loud on *Panorama*!'

Children and adults alike watched *Swap Shop*. They loved the show's disorderly atmosphere. Noel's copresenter Keith Chegwin, who joined the second series along with Noel's friend John Craven, was always mobbed by kids at his travelling Swaporamas. Recalling his first meeting with his *Swap Shop* copresenter, Keith revealed he was shocked at Noel's vanity. 'I wandered over to Noel and we had a very brief chat, after which he asked if I had a pen and paper so that he could give me his autograph,' said Cheggers. 'I was utterly gobsmacked. I thought, This is how the other half live: superstars trading autographs with each other. But he wasn't too keen on asking for mine!'

*Swap Shop* was the show that introduced the telly phone-in. Noel would be talking to a movie star or pop idol and would invite the audience to give them a ring. The Post Office, who at that time ran the telephone network, was not amused. Noel explains, 'The first time we invited listeners to call in, we waited and waited and hardly anyone called up. We thought nobody was watching. But what had actually happened was that all the kids had called up at the same time and jammed the system. The Post Office went mad because we'd locked up a number of telephone exchanges in London's West End. There were high-level meetings to discuss how they could get emergency calls through.'

Noel, whose lurid multicoloured shirts and jumpers that

he wore on the show became legendary, acknowledges how important *Swap Shop* was to his later success. 'It was the foundation stone of my career. It not only gave me experience of live TV: it gave me a link to the family audience. The people who watched *Swap Shop* now tune into *Noel's House Party*. None of us involved in the show thought it would be quite so big, although we all had our hopes and dreams.' He deliberately didn't make any concessions to the kids – he treated them as equals. 'I try to think of them as adult persons who happen to be on the short side, and are sometimes a little lacking in experience.'

Mike Smith was in regular contact with Noel during the period when he was making the transition into television, and tells how Noel was 'picked out' by one of the BBC's most influential men, Bill Cotton. Bill Cotton became Managing Director of BBC Television and was honoured with a BAFTA Fellowship Award in 1998 for his contribution to TV. He is credited with masterminding the careers of Bruce Forsyth, The Two Ronnies, Morecambe and Wise and Noel Edmonds. Mike says, 'Noel was singled out by Bill Cotton when he was Head of Entertainment. He marked out Noel and guided his career in TV and made him into the star that he is today. He was the most important person in his career.

'Noel was still at Radio 1. He was changing from the *Breakfast Show* back to Sunday mornings, but the radio was taking more of a back seat. His TV career was immense.'

As a television star, Noel found himself in the spotlight to a far greater degree than he had ever known. He loved the limelight and enjoyed the feeling of importance and worth that fame brought him. He had worked hard to get where he was and now he was able to reap some of the rewards, like expensive fast cars for himself, such as a Ford GT 40 and a Jaguar XJS, and, in 1977, a brown Rolls-Royce Silver Shadow for his beloved father.

Paul Burnett recalls: 'Noel's dad had always dreamt of driving a Rolls-Royce but was the headmaster of a school and couldn't afford to buy one himself. Noel bought him one as a surprise and dropped the keys into his hand and said, "There's your car outside." His dad was really thrilled and I think Noel was quite moved by that.'

Burnett explains how Noel was able to make the most of his well-respected position at the BBC to get his own way. He says, 'Television initially goes against everything that radio disc jockeys are. They have to know everything you are going to say; everything is scripted; everything is Autocued: stand there and look this way. But, because Noel was a top DJ on Radio 1 when he was approached to do *Swap Shop*, he had the clout to be able to say, "Yes, OK, but this is how I want it done. I want to be able to leap off the stage and go into the audience at a moment's notice if I feel like doing it, and the camera follows me." And it coincided with the new lightweight cameras and the mobility of cameras. Noel actually exploited that and made it work. He was the first to introduce that kind of radio DJ spontaneity to television. I think he just thought that was the way it should be done, and of course it was very successful. I don't think it is really recognised that the Chris Evanses and Chris Tarrants of this world owe something of a debt to Noel.'

Burnett also noticed how all-embracing his friend's fame had become when they met up for lunch not long after Noel had begun working in television: 'I have always thought that the nice thing about radio fame is that with it comes a certain amount of anonymity. Once Noel became "telly famous" I noticed how different his life became. We would be with him having lunch and people would quite happily come over. They wouldn't mean to be rude, but of course it was very intrusive. They'd stare and say things that they wouldn't dream of saying to anybody else. They didn't have any regard for his feelings. They'd say out loud, "Oh, he's shorter than I thought he was!" I don't know about Noel, but it would bother the life out of me.

'I don't think fame sits comfortably with him. I think if

you really lap it up then it's great, but if you don't, if you are naturally quite a private person, which I think Noel is, then it can be very difficult.'

As well as the problems caused by being recognised wherever he went, Noel realised that, as his fame grew, so did the press's interest in him. Fame, of course, is a double-edged sword. Noel was only too happy to cooperate with interviews when he wanted to promote himself or publicise his motor-racing interests, but he found it harder to cope with the fact that his private life was open to scrutiny. Even his beard was questioned and discussed. 'I use it for dusting records and keeping morsels of tasty food handy for a snack,' he jokingly replied when asked why he had one. Gill was also asked what her opinion of it was. 'It is so much part of Noel I almost forget it's on his chin,' she said. 'I would certainly miss it if he shaved it off. He shampoos it regularly and keeps it so soft. I just don't notice it when he kisses me.'

However, Noel has always managed to ensure that the media gets to know only what he wants them to know. He has cleverly managed his publicity in such a way that, really, very little is known about him on a personal level. This is borne out by the fact that, throughout virtually the whole of 1976 and 1977, his marriage was on the rocks but the newspapers didn't find out. During that time, Noel was regularly appearing on the television and the radio and still being written about, but his happy banter on the air belied the trouble he was having behind the scenes. He managed to keep from the press the fact that he and Gill had separated, and that, while his career was going from strength to strength, his personal life was in disarray.

In fact, Noel was seeing another woman, a relationship that he had begun in 1975. But the adept way that Noel handled his publicity in those days meant that his version of events was not challenged. The way Noel has it, he and Gill broke up for a year because of the pressures of his fame. He made no mention of the other woman in his life.

The first inkling that the outside world had of any disharmony in Noel's marriage was in April 1977 when Gill ended up in hospital after an overdose. Police broke into the couple's country cottage in the tiny village of Preston St Mary, Suffolk, after being alerted by a gardener. They found 27-year-old Gill lying on her bed unconscious. Noel was telephoned and he raced from the Radio 1 studio in London to the West Suffolk Hospital in Bury St Edmunds. His wife was given medical treatment and kept in overnight before being allowed home. Speaking to the press a few days later, she denied she had intended to harm herself. She also denied that their five-year marriage was in trouble. She said, 'I know a lot of people are saying our marriage is on the rocks and I took an overdose, but nothing could be further from the truth. I took some pills for a tummy upset but they only made me feel worse. I lay on the bed and I just couldn't move. I remember the gardener and his wife arriving but I couldn't get up and let them in. They were obviously a bit alarmed and they called the police. It was a complete accident. There is nothing wrong between Noel and me.'

Gill did not tell her parents about her overdose and Geoffrey and Margaret Slater didn't hear about it from their son-in-law either. Instead, they heard it from a friend of Gill's. It was a bewildering and worrying time for them. Mr Slater explains: 'I never got to the bottom of what had happened, except that one imagines she'd got so upset about things generally and her marriage going wrong that she took an overdose. That's all I can think of. We didn't know all the details but I suppose we just jumped to that conclusion.'

Gill's overdose, accident or not, caused shock among their friends. Chris Fone recalls: 'Those of us who knew her never believed that she would do something like that on purpose. It just didn't stack up. It was not in character.'

But it turned out that Mr and Mrs Slater had hit the nail on the head with their guess about their daughter's marriage problems. For, six months later, in October 1977, Noel admitted to the press that he and Gill had been separated for almost a year, but followed it up with the happy announcement that they were hoping to get back together. In a double-page spread in the *Daily Mirror* Noel revealed: 'HOW MY HEARTBREAK SECRET HAS ENDED IN HAPPINESS'. He admitted: 'Gill and I have been living apart for almost a year. We saw each other frequently until about four months ago, but then we realised that what we were trying to do in terms of saving our marriage just wasn't working out. For two and a half months we didn't see each other at all. Gill never listened to my radio show and avoided seeing me on television or reading about me. I think she missed me and, by God, I missed her.'

Noel's parents were absolutely distraught by the turn of events in their son's marriage. They never once allowed themselves to think that the break might be final, and, according to Noel, quite deliberately steered him and Gill back together.

'What caused the trouble was a total lack of communication between us,' Noel said. 'The strains of my business – show business – aggravated things. I just hadn't realised that my success was so extensive and that Gill was being pushed into the background more and more. That won't happen again. I am rethinking my entire career, especially my work on radio.'

The news of trouble in the Edmonds' marriage led some commentators to dub the *Breakfast Show* the 'Break-up Show', because Noel was the second host to experience marital difficulties: Tony Blackburn's marriage to Tessa Wyatt didn't survive his stint on the show.

Noel said he and Gill had sat down to discuss their future and decided to give their marriage another go. They decided to sell their Suffolk home and buy a new dream home, and Noel promised that she would no longer come second to his career. 'A year ago I couldn't have put my hand on my heart and told you that I would give up everything in my career for the sake of my marriage,' he said. 'But I could now. Gill wouldn't want me to do that but if it was necessary I could.

I have decided what I want out of life and right at the top of the list is a happy marriage.

'From the start I was too soft when people were rude to her. For example, she found the young girls hanging around me easy to cope with until she was physically pushed to one side by them at discos or at shop openings. I was guilty of not protecting her enough. I was able to cope with the professional side of my life without realising how it was eroding my personal life. There were occasions when I wondered whether it was worth going through all that agony, whether I should put this one down to experience. But those thoughts never lasted more than a few seconds. I have never stopped loving her, you see, and I cannot imagine not being married to her. Unfortunately, if you are married for six years the gloss does wear off and you tend to start taking the other person for granted. I don't think we will be living apart for much longer. We will be back together soon because it is getting more and more painful each time we say goodbye.'

What Noel had failed to mention in this confessional outpouring of emotion was that he had been involved with another woman, a 24-year-old redhead called Patricia Askew. Two days later, a hurt and bewildered Patricia told of her shock when she read about the Edmonds' reconciliation in the paper. 'I loved him dearly,' she said. 'But I can't imagine that I would ever want to become closely involved with him again. I'm not bitter but I am very hurt that he announced he was going back to Gill without even telling me first. The first I knew was when he rang me to apologise about the way the news was broken in the press. I was awfully upset and so were my parents, because we had a serious relationship. I don't want to use the word "affair", because it makes it sound so sordid and we never set up home together.'

Noel's father-in-law believed the star was cheating on Gill with other women and a serious rift developed between Noel and his parents-in-law. Mr Slater recalls how Noel's treatment of his daughter drove a bitter wedge between them: 'It ended up that we didn't get on. The way he was living and treating our daughter upset us as well as upsetting her. It was a very, very difficult time and it all ended up very tragically and in great tearfulness. I was highly disappointed because we were very fond of Noel and liked him enormously.'

Mr Slater was in no doubt what was causing the problems in his daughter's marriage. 'He was playing the field. We heard things from other people and his parents, with whom we were friendly. We heard it from Gill's sister as well as through the grapevine. There was no getting away from it. Gill used to get girls going round to the house and pestering him. And then she'd find out that he'd been out with them. So it wasn't difficult to find out. They were groupies and she was convinced he had taken it one stage further. The whole thing got very uptight, very stressful, very, very silly, and for three years we hardly saw our own daughter, not because of anything she had done. We had a phone call from him one night and I blew my top and he blew his top. We were trading insults. He accused me of saying various things which I hadn't said, of not helping in their relationship. But you just want to see your own daughter happy.'

Because of their rift with Noel, Geoffrey and Margaret Slater's only communication with Gill was through her sister, Hilary. It wasn't until years later that Gill finally admitted to her parents that Noel's infidelities were the cause of their marriage problems. When her husband and her parents, who had once been so close, fell out, Gill loyally stuck by her husband.

Geoffrey Slater says, 'That period was just pretty horrific for both of us. Before this we had seen our daughter every week or two and we put her decision not to see us down to her hoping that the situation was going to resolve itself. I think Gill still had a basic love and loyalty to him and didn't like to think that we had fallen out and that she was piggy-in-the-middle. It was very difficult. She eventually confirmed he had been playing the field when she came back to us.'

Patricia Askew, a secretary for a record company, described Noel as 'wonderful, warm and generous'. She said, 'We became extremely close because I knew his wife very well and he used to confide in me. I was a shoulder he could cry on and he would pour out his troubles to me. I was his closest confidante and all the friends in our circle knew we were going out together over a long period. My parents know I won't be seeing him again and they are quite distressed too. Noel's relationship with his wife has been an on–off affair for many months and I suppose he wanted the best of all worlds by having me as a good friend. I tried some time ago to get him to release details of his marital difficulties and our friendship. But he just told me to leave it to his public-relations manager.'

Noel was furious when Patricia spoke out. Although he had spoken to the press about his marital problems, he was unhappy when Patricia did the same. Noel was exposed as having been economical with the truth in his interview with the *Daily Mirror*. And, by making their affair public, Patricia could have jeopardised Noel's reconciliation with Gill. He moved fast, hinting that their relationship was partly the product of Patricia's imagination. He said, 'Patricia is an excellent friend of mine and still is. I am amazed she has talked in these terms to a total stranger rather than to me. I think she has read more into our relationship than there really has been. I shall have to ring her to discuss this whole thing.

'Patricia is part of my inner circle and I have confided in her and I suppose you could say we have been very close friends. I do not want her hurt, and it was because of the rumours circulating about people I have been seen out with that I decided to make public the problems in my marriage. Gill is aware of all my friends and I am now confident that my marriage can withstand the publicity.' He said that when he and his wife separated they both realised they could meet someone else. 'It was a risk we took, but nothing like that happened. The main thing now is that nothing can prise Gill and I apart.'

Gill stood by her man, saying, 'There were so many pressures I could not bear it. Apart from the girls pestering Noel, he was having to work seven days a week. But I have always loved Noel and he has always loved me. As soon as we can find a nice house, preferably outside London, we will put everything behind us.'

On the subject of children, Noel had previously admitted, 'I'm a monster who hates babies. I can't stand the way they cry and yell all the time. Even holding a baby could bring me out in a rash. Maybe I'm allergic to them. Fortunately my wife Gill feels the same as I do.' Mindful not to upset his growing army of young fans, he added, 'I've got millions of other people's kids, and that's great.' But now, as he grew older, fatherhood no longer appeared so daunting. Perhaps a baby was just what they needed to cement their relationship. Noel announced: 'Gill and I are now envisaging starting a family. For the first time, we have talked about what we want, about kids, about the future, about everything. We are really going to try hard and we have every confidence.'

Once he had decided to make his marriage work, Noel put all his energies into making things right between him and Gill. He announced that he planned to give up the *Breakfast Show*, leaving him with more time to devote to his television career and his wife, and he scoured the Home Counties for a suitable house for them. Five months later, in March 1978, Noel found his dream home, the Manor House, situated in the affluent Buckinghamshire hamlet of Weston Turville. It was a stunningly beautiful Queen Anne house set on the site of a Norman castle, and Noel fell head over heels in love with it. He paid £100,000 for the mansion, which was built in 1730. It boasted seven bedrooms and three bathrooms, as well as two separate cottages, a tennis court, immaculately manicured gardens and its own moat. It was set in ten acres of grounds, where Noel, who had always loathed London, found release from the stresses and strains of his life. From the moment that he glimpsed the Manor House through the trees on his way home from the BBC studios, Noel would begin to unwind. The white farm gate would swing open at the touch of a button and his car would crunch down the gravel drive, past manicured lawns and white doves fluttering peacefully around the dovecote. He spent all his spare time working on the farm, rejoicing in being out in the fresh air, miles away from the dirt and congestion of London. 'I love grass and hate city life,' he said. 'No one belives me, but my two greatest interests are decorating and gardening.'

But the Manor House had rather a lot of grass. 'Farmer Edmonds' solved that by buying four bullocks and a couple of heifers, but, true to form, made sure they would be a good investment. 'With beef prices going up all the time they're worth a lot more than I paid for them,' he said triumphantly. Noel enthusiastically set to work with a spot of DIY, renovating the Manor's bedrooms and bathrooms, and happily proclaimed, 'I've vowed to be carried out of it feet first, in a box.'

In January, Noel did what he'd promised Gill and quit the *Breakfast Show*. 'I have done it for five years,' he said. 'And that's a long time. You reach a point when you can't give the programme any more.' He would spend his mornings making love to his wife, he said. 'We'd very much like to have kids of our own, and with the new house we have got an area where we can start thinking about a family.'

He was replaced by Dave Lee Travis, DLT to his fans. Noel was clearly glad to give up the early mornings. Ceremoniously smashing up his alarm clock with a hammer, he enthused, 'People said it would take me months to adjust to normal living – it took me three days. Instead of rising at 5 a.m. I lie back, think of the bad old days and go back to sleep until 8.30 a.m. When I get up I never listen to the radio. People I have known for a long time see a difference in me. They remark that my eyes have changed colour. A month ago they were a shocking shade of red; now they are blue and they sparkle. That sounds daft, but they do. My whole life seems to sparkle all the time.'

Gill was asked if she had any advice for DLT's wife Marianne and an outpouring of bitterness ensued. 'They will have to give up any thoughts of a decent social life and definitely forget about having children,' she said. 'I gave it to Marianne straight. We had a long heart-to-heart talk and I warned her not to get a chip on her shoulder, the way I did.' Five years of living with the host of the *Breakfast Show* had clearly got to Gill. She continued, 'I told her she would have to get used to taking second place to the job. God, I got so fed up with being the old misery who always had to leave a party at ten o'clock because Noel had to get to bed early. In the end it was easier to refuse invitations than go through the awful business of explaining why we had to leave so that Noel could be up at 5 a.m. the next morning.'

Their love life had also begun to suffer, she said. 'In the beginning, Noel would come home from work in the afternoon and we would go to bed. Then he started taking on more and more work and eventually he wasn't getting home until late at night. He would go straight to sleep and then be off early next morning. Life became one long treadmill. And I couldn't have coped with trying to keep a child quiet while Daddy got his much needed sleep.'

Both Gill and Noel were adamant that his giving up the *Breakfast Show* would make everything right. That July, the couple celebrated their seventh wedding anniversary, something that, twelve months before, neither had thought they would get to. Noel decided to mark the occasion with a really special gift. Gill's one extravagant dream was to own an E-Type Jaguar, and at 6 a.m. on the morning of their wedding anniversary she looked out of the bedroom window and saw the car on the lawn. 'I had it delivered late at night and put it on the lawn with the message "I LOVE YOU" in large letters stuck across it,' said Noel proudly. He had also splashed out on an extravagant present for himself – his own helicopter.

If anything, Noel's television career was proving to be even more successful than his radio career. *Swap Shop* was phenomenally successful and he also presented *Hobby Horse* – a children's version of *Mastermind* – and *Lucky Numbers*, where the show's editor, Rosemary Gill, said of Noel, 'He can seem a chillingly ambitious man.' It was an off-the-cuff remark that has haunted Noel for almost twenty years, and one that he found extremely hurtful. 'It made me sound like a Nazi,' he complained bitterly.

In addition, he made his television directing debut with *Ten, Nine, Eight*, a programme that looked behind the TV scenes and that he also presented. 'I found it completely different and quite an alarming experience,' he admitted. 'And I can confess that as a presenter I make a bally awful director. It has given me a new appreciation of what television directors do, and how hard their jobs are. It is much easier being on the performer's end of the camera.'

Noel was also still working for Radio 1 and had gone back to doing the three-hour Sunday-morning show as well as hosting an hour-long radio chat show called *Talkabout* on Thursday evenings. It was while listening to the Sunday-morning programme that the nation was first introduced to Hissing Sid, the fictional antihero of Keith Michell's record, 'Captain Beaky'. Noel heard the record on *Junior Choice* and played it on his show, sparking an outbreak of Beakymania that swept the country. Hissing Sid, the record claimed, was a snake who was supposed to have swallowed one of Beaky's band, Timid Toad. Noel received on average 3,000 letters a week on the topic: is Hissing Sid guilty or innocent? He even broadcast the trial of Hissing Sid on his show. 'I thought it was wonderful,' he said. 'I played it on my Sunday-morning show and was swamped by queries and requests for more. I had no idea it was going to turn out like this. The characters have caught people's imaginations somehow and the response is incredible. Last week I came out of Broadcasting House after finishing the Sunday show to find a group of Beaky Freakies complete with banners and placards. As I was chatting to them, a police car with a flashing blue light drew up and a burly policeman got out. He strode towards me and I got this cold flush, wondering what I had done wrong and thinking how embarrassing it was in front of all these people. Then he said, "Excuse me, sir, but I have reason to believe you can help us with our inquiry. We're trying to find Hissing Sid." That made me realise just how big the whole Beaky thing is. Even the police are in on it!'

As well as providing the nation with a dose of what he described as 'well-needed silliness', Noel's hobbies were also occupying a lot of his time. His love affair with motor racing had started to wane after a few unpleasant experiences with other drivers. 'Motor racing isn't really a sport any more,' he complained. 'People take it far too seriously. That's why I gave it up. I got fed up with being pushed off the track by people who would stop at nothing to win. That's not sport. Whereas I was perfectly happy not to get involved in private races with other drivers, a couple of guys appeared to take exception to me. I was often lucky to get past the first corner, as they would do all they could to push me off.' He now preferred the thrill of the water and the excitement of powerboat racing: 'The boats look so graceful when they are skimming across the water that you would never realise that the people inside are getting shaken apart. Every time you hit a wave it is like being kicked in the back by a horse. I couldn't believe just how painful it can be until I first went out in a rough sea. But the noise, the vibration and the gut-wrenching sensation when you are bouncing from one wave crest to the next is all part of the thrill. Powerboating is much more fun than motor racing. Powerboating is different. People stop to help another boat if it gets into real trouble during a race. I have made a lot of friends since I started powerboating. I made very few friends motor racing.'

One of those friends was millionaire businessman Ray McEnhill, who owned *Miss Pearl*, the boat Noel raced in. Another was Derek James, the two having patched up their argument over the cheque incident. James says, 'In 1976 I was in the Hilton having a drink with David Hamilton and Noel was there. David suggested we go over and have a chat with him, so we did, and Noel was actually very civilised. I said it was bloody stupid our not talking to one another because I'd actually got a lot of bookings I could pass his way. He said he'd ring me in the morning during the show. I thought he probably wouldn't, but he did, and that's where it struck up from.

'I used to arrange most of his nightclub appearances for him and he liked the fact that he didn't have to worry about the money. I would arrange the fee and I was always at each event. He liked that because it meant he didn't have to deal with anybody else. It led eventually, of course, to him saying I might as well handle everything. He relied very heavily on me. We had a tremendous rapport. He would say to me – the only flattering thing he ever said – that he had never had anybody do so many things for him. Noel has never had a manager: he always used to say to me, "You are not my manager; you are my business partner." We ran all his affairs under the broad umbrella of Manor House Consultants, which involved anything from buying things he wanted for the farm to arranging his bookings. You name it, we did it. At one stage, my assistant and I used to handle his fan mail and everything. We used to literally wipe his boots for him.'

But, Derek says, he soon began to realise that there was a downside to working for Noel. 'We had a lot of fun and I got him quite a lot of big money in those early days, but I just felt that, the more you did, the more he wanted. You didn't get any real sort of gratitude. Gill waited on him hand and foot but I think he is just one of those people who, the more you do for him, the less he respects you.'

Derek couldn't help but notice how obsessed Noel was by

business and how he longed to emulate his highly successful friend Ray McEnhill: 'The one undying passion Noel has – and I think he still suffers from today – is that he sees himself as a big entrepreneurial businessman. But he isn't a Richard Branson by any stretch of the imagination. He has got this desire to be a big tycoon and that's his undoing, because he launches these things in a fit of pique and goes 500 per cent at it and can't see the pitfalls in front of him. I think it was meeting Ray that fired up the idea of him being a businessman. He admired his skills. Ray had this big oceangoing yacht which was like a mini *Britannia*, lots of trappings, and I think Noel got a bit of green eye there and wanted to emulate that. When Noel first got his helicopter he didn't own it all – it was his and Ray's. Ray was quite happy to half-fund it and take a back seat – in fact, he never even used it.'

Derek was set to work trying to find a sponsor for the powerboat that Noel and Ray raced in. He recalls, 'It is quite a dangerous sport and you've got to throw lots of serious money at it to get anywhere. They wanted to attract more attention to themselves and get a sponsor. It was a three-man crew – navigator, driver and throttle man. Noel went in as navigator. The first year, Olympus Pearlcorder sponsored it; and the second year I secured a deal with Cossack hairspray, which was rather perverse really because out of the crew only Noel had any hair – Ray McEnhill was bald as a coot. So we had a bright-red boat with COSSACK HAIRSPRAY on the side, with a very motley crew on board.

'It was quite fun at times but hell at others. I would be piggy-in-the-middle and when the muck hit the fan it was, "Oh, Derek, go and sort that one out."'

As he earned more and more money Noel didn't forget his parents. As well as the Rolls-Royce he had bought for his father, Noel got Derek James to line up extravagant treats for them. Derek says, 'Lydia doted on Noel. I used to laugh because she was always very bossy, you know: "My Noel's going to do this." I will always remember the year that he went right over the top on Christmas presents. He got me to get a round of golf with Tony Jacklin for her, which I did, and a game of bowls with the bowls champion for his father. And he flew them to New York on Concorde as a treat.'

But Noel's great dream was to beat the world waterspeed record. In the spring of 1981 he met a man with whom he thought he could make this dream a reality. The businessman Basil Wainwright and Noel set up a company to build a futuristic 'hydro-wing' craft named *Excalibur*. The boat would be capable of speeds up to 300 mph and Noel planned to pilot it on Coniston Water in the Lake District that summer. The scheme was bigger and more ambitious than anything Noel had been involved with before, and, significantly, he was investing a large amount of his own money.

It was a calamitous mistake which was to take him to the brink of financial ruin. Noel was about to taste failure for the first time in his life.

# **6** Trials and Tribulations

T
HE BASIL WAINWRIGHT affair, which had started so promisingly, ended in total humiliation for Noel. On 15 June 1981, the star, ever one to do things in style, held a lavish press conference at the Savoy Hotel in London where he announced to the waiting media his grand plan to beat the world waterspeed record by building and piloting the fastest powerboat on the planet. By his side was Wainwright, his business partner in the venture, and on the table before them was a glittering model of their planned revolutionary speedboat, *Excalibur*. The project, which would cost £500,000, represented far more to Noel than just a hobby. With it, he planned to gain recognition as a speedboat racer and make his fortune into the bargain. 'I want to show people that I'm more than someone who appears on radio and TV,' he said. 'I have been very, very lucky with my broadcasting career. To achieve that success you have got to have ego and want to be famous. I think I've achieved that now, but I'm not a millionaire and what I want to achieve with Project Hydro-Wing is commercial success.'

By this time, Noel had added hosting the BBC motoring programme *Top Gear* to his workload, and he had met Basil Wainwright and designer Frederick Stidworthy when they appeared on the show. Noel had told them his idea for a revolutionary boat design, and Noel and Wainwright formed a company called Creaseglen Limited. The plan was that Stidworthy would design the boat and it would be built in Wainwright's factory in Redditch, in the West Midlands. If successful, it would be sold around the world, making them all rich. The project was to be financed jointly by Wainwright's company and Noel's own bank account. 'I am putting in £100,000 of my own money,' he said at the press launch. 'And I can assure you that will hurt. But I regard the money as venture capital. I'm not throwing it away. I like to think I'm a businessman.'

But Noel may just have well thrown it away, or chucked it overboard, for Basil Wainwright was a crook. Just one month later, Noel's *Excalibur* dream was in tatters when it transpired that smooth-talking Wainwright had embezzled £70,000 of his money. The police were called in and Noel faced up to the grim truth that he had been taken for a mug. For, if Wainwright was a fraud, then Noel was guilty of being naive to say the least. He had let his dream of sporting stardom override his better judgement. Derek James couldn't believe how gullible Noel was. Noel, who had always been so sharp with money when it came to negotiating pay deals and promoting himself, displayed an astonishing lack of wisdom by entrusting a complete stranger with what was then an enormous sum of money. James says, 'I think Noel was very naive about this. I couldn't believe that they had a joint account. I don't think Noel was even a signatory to it, and huge amounts of money were being handed over to this project. I didn't think it was a good idea but nonetheless I had to go along with it and I actually masterminded the press conference at the Savoy. The project had a lot of merit. It was actually quite a sound idea, but this guy stitched him up something rotten.'

James reveals the bizarre way in which Noel first discovered that all was not as it seemed: 'It was the time of Prince Charles and Diana's wedding and we discovered that the address on some adverts in the colour supplements for Royal Wedding memorabilia plates was exactly the same as the address Wainwright was using in the Midlands.' This set Noel wondering what exactly Wainwright was up to and, inevitably, what had happened to the money he had deposited in Creaseglen Ltd's bank account. When Wainwright refused to let him see the company accounts, Noel went to Redditch to have it out with him. The two had a fierce row, which was captured by the BBC camera crew Noel had taken with him to film the confrontation. He released a statement to the press, saying that he was 'requesting that Basil Wainwright returns to me immediately £70,000'. Wainwright hit back by announcing his intention to sue Noel for £1.25 million and serving him with a writ claiming defamation of character and damage to commercial projects. But days later he was arrested and charged with theft.

At his trial at Worcester Crown Court in May 1983, Wainwright was found guilty of twenty-two charges: nine of theft, five of false accounting, five of forgery and three of obtaining money by deception, and was jailed for three years. Judge John Lee told Wainwright, who had denied all the charges, that more than £100,000 had disappeared because of his 'thoroughly dishonest' activities. It was clear that more offences had been committed than were contained in the charges brought, he added.

During the five-week trial, the jury heard how Noel invested £70,000 in the *Excalibur* project but lost every penny because Wainwright had spent the money on trips to America, a BMW car, his telephone bill and a new bathroom at his home. The BBC had planned to make a film of the project called *The Birth of a Boat*, the court was told, when instead it should have been called *The Boat That Never Was*. The prosecution alleged that the scheme had been a wholesale fraud 'almost from the word go' and that Noel had been 'taken for a complete ride'. The court heard that Noel even had dreams of becoming Sir Noel Edmonds. Judge Lee said, 'His dream was to become the new Donald Campbell – with perhaps a knighthood later.'

It was hugely embarrassing for Noel. He told the court that he had raised the £70,000 with a bank overdraft and had allowed the money to be withdrawn from Creaseglen's account on cheques signed only by Wainwright. He had been taken in by the 49-year-old, who, according to the prosecution, was 'an impressive personality holding doctorates and specialising in engineering and doctorates'.

'I've been a real pillock and I don't mind admitting it,' Noel said after the trial. 'What a wally I have been to fall for someone like that. Everyone is allowed one mistake. At least I'm not out on the street like some people might have been.' Noel couldn't even claim that he'd been picked out by Wainwright. 'He didn't find me; I found him,' he said ruefully. 'It came out in the court case that he hadn't even targeted me. He couldn't believe his luck when "guess who" came through the door.'

Most people probably thought that he could well afford the loss. After all, he was a rich television and radio star. But Noel was putting on a brave face to mask the seriousness of the situation. In fact, the whole affair brought him perilously close to financial ruin.

Noel learnt a bitter lesson at the hands of Basil Wainwright, one that he was determined not to repeat. Never again would he jeopardise the lifestyle he had worked so hard for. In his later business deals the only significant money that Noel would be supplying would be in the form of his own bankability as a celebrity 'name'. He still has the model of *Excalibur*. Most people would have thrown it in the bin and tried to put the whole sorry business behind them, but Noel kept it as a sobering reminder of his foolishness. 'The model of the boat is all I have left out of that particular experience,' he says. 'It sits in a display cupboard right in the middle of the house. I walk past it every day – Noel's Folly! My pride was dented, yes. I lost a lot of money, but mistakes are to be remembered and learnt from. Not to be shuffled under the carpet.'

The year 1981 was a difficult one for Noel. In July he had discovered the unpalatable truth about Wainwright and lost an enormous sum of money, and two months later he was forced to admit defeat in another area of his life: his marriage was finally over.

Noel had begun seeing Patricia Askew again. This was well known by those in his immediate circle, and this time he and Gill couldn't reconcile their differences. Noel left Gill at the end of August and moved into a house in London where Patricia was a frequent visitor. 'There is no chance of reconciliation,' he said. 'I guess we have just fallen out of love. It is a tragedy for both of us.'

They had tried desperately to make things work, he said, but had decided to divorce: 'When we got together again after our separation five years ago, we fought to save our marriage and we tried very hard. You can't throw bricks at people who have tried to save their marriages, but it has become clear over the last eighteen months that we don't have the right feelings towards each other. We don't have any more that closeness and understanding that a good marriage ought to have.'

The marriage break-up came as no surprise to those who knew Noel. His parents knew their son's marriage was in trouble again – and why – as did Mr and Mrs Slater.

Geoffrey Slater says, 'We heard from our other daughter about him playing the field. Gill didn't discuss it with us at the time, the chief reason being that she was embarrassed about it, I think. It wasn't until some time after their divorce that she confided in us about it. She was angry about him playing around with these other women. I don't know if she ever confronted them. Sometimes they both had to shoo them away. But marriages don't break up because schoolgirls knock on the door. It was certainly much more than that.'

Much closer to the situation at that time was Derek James. It was he who found Noel the London house that the star used for liaisons with Patricia Askew, and he remembers Noel's manner when he finally left Gill. 'His attitude was, I'm out and I'm not going back,' says Derek. 'He wouldn't even go back to pick up his shirts.'

Patricia, known as Trish to her friends, had dyed her red hair and was now a peroxide blonde. As well as changing her hair, she had also changed her mind about never wanting to be close to Noel again, which was what she had said when he went back to Gill five years before. According to friends, Noel was crazy about her, and when he wanted to rekindle their affair she agreed.

Derek James says, 'I found him a place, a bolt hole, in Queensdale Place, Holland Park. It was rented, and it fitted him mainly when he split up with Gill. It was during the time we had the house that Noel brought Trish back into the frame. Trish didn't exactly live with him at Queensdale Place: she would just pop round. He was potty over her. I remember her being fairly thin – he likes his ladies thin – and a real blonde bombshell.'

But Noel played his cards close to his chest. He said at the time, 'Very few people know what I'm doing, or with whom, and I enjoy that. I am very happy just to keep that to myself.'

Derek adds, 'I always got the feeling that Noel treated Gill very badly. She literally waited on him hand and foot and I think she got the same treatment that I did: the more you did for him the less respect he had for you. Also, I know he wanted children and whether Gill couldn't, or wouldn't, I don't know.'

Indeed, Noel has said, 'The reason we separated was very simple. It was over the subject of whether we wanted to have children or not. We are two people who grew apart and had different ambitions. You ask yourself, Do I want to grow old with this person? Do I want to be alone with her? If two people are able to hold each other and say, "This isn't right," you've got to come to terms with it eventually. We had a friendship and a loyalty to each other so it was a very difficult time for both of us. I know it is a cliché but we are still friends. We don't see each other but we correspond.'

Gill refuses to talk about her ex-husband to this day, but her father says he didn't accept the excuse about children: 'I think that might have been a smokescreen.' Also, according to her father, it is not the case that Gill and Noel are still friends. 'To my knowledge they haven't seen or spoken to each other for years,' he said. 'I wouldn't have thought she has any warm feelings about him at all.'

Derek James agrees that 'it wasn't an amicable split'. And other friends confirm that, contrary to Noel's insistence of a friendly break-up, Gill was left full of bitterness.

Gill's and Noel's parents were also casualties of the divorce. Geoffrey and Margaret Slater were disappointed because they had once been very fond of Noel and liked him enormously; and Dudley and Lydia were distressed at the loss of their daughter-in-law. Geoffrey Slater reveals: 'Noel's parents loved Gill and they were very sympathetic about what had happened. They have stayed reasonably friendly over all this, and Gill is still in contact with Noel's mother. They phone each other occasionally. His father was highly instrumental in educating Noel and also in guiding him, and he relied on his father a lot. He was always going to his father for advice. He was very much his mentor and I think his father was very bitterly disappointed that they split up, and so was his mother. They both got on very well with Gill.'

Accepting that his marriage was over was hard for Noel. He said recently, 'I look back on Gill with considerable sympathy. She had to handle my ambition, which was worse then. She saw me through this difficult time where I was being offered fantastic jobs and very large sums of money, but I was committed to getting the *Breakfast Show* right. When it was finished I looked around and saw we didn't have a lot in common any more. But I kept going with the relationship because I didn't want to admit to failure. I'd never failed at anything.'

At the time, he confessed it had been hard putting on an act at work. 'It has been very difficult in recent weeks to appear bright and cheerful on radio and TV while all this has been going on,' he said. 'I think I'm the fortunate one out of the two of us. Gill's the one who hasn't got the work to do. I've got lots of work and plenty of things to keep me busy and that always helps when you're down. And I have never felt so depressed in my whole life.'

Noel and Gill were divorced less than a year later, on 18 October 1982 – eleven years and three months after their wedding. Gill was granted a decree nisi at the London Divorce Court on the grounds of her husband's admitted adultery. He refused to name the other woman cited in the divorce petition, but was still tanned from the holiday he had recently taken with Patricia Askew in the Seychelles.

When Noel left her, Gill continued living in their house in Weston Turville. But Noel wanted his beloved home back, and early in 1982 she moved into a cottage in the village and Noel took up residence in the Manor House. Gill was just a few minutes' walk away, an arrangement which, according to Noel, suited them both. 'The fact that we live in the same village suits us – neither of us is planning to move,' he said immediately after his divorce. 'Living here in the village, meeting and talking with each other, gives us both a great deal of happiness and pleasure. I understand now that divorce can be much easier if there is hate. But there is no hate between me and Gill and there never has been. We both still care a great deal about each other, and about each other's career, and we meet regularly and talk two or three times a week over the telephone.' But weeks later Noel had installed Patricia in the Manor House, and Gill later left the village and moved away.

In January 1982, Noel had announced he was quitting *Swap Shop* after 6 years and 146 shows. At its peak, it had attracted 10 million viewers, making it the most successful children's programme in history. 'I want to move on and find a new direction,' said Noel. 'I firmly believe that the time to do that is just when things are going so well that everybody expects you to stay where you are. In the last six years I have become a national figure. I have public recognition, which is nice, and personal accomplishments, which are also very nice. I have my farm, a helicopter and money in the bank. In view of the fact that I owe it all to *Swap Shop*, I will be very sad to leave it.'

He had thought about quitting the year before but had decided to stay on and help the show fight the ITV opposition, *Tiswas*. 'Now that we've taken them apart and we are once again all-powerful on Saturdays, I can't think of a better time to leave,' he said. The show's editor, Rosemary Gill, said they hadn't had time to think of the future without Noel, and in the event Noel's final day in March 1982 was *Swap Shop*'s last, too. The show was just too closely identified with Noel for them to consider getting another presenter, said the BBC.

Noel was still hosting his Sunday-morning Radio 1 show, but the writing was on the wall for that because he had grown restless. He now realised his future lay exclusively in television. 'Live television is my strong point,' he acknowledged. 'I'd like to stick with it. I have always been a BBC man, but if ITV came up with the right idea I would consider swapping channels. My main concern is to do something interesting. If I can't, I'll stop broadcasting.' His remarks were aimed directly at the BBC and the message was clear: Give me something good, or I'm off. It was a ploy he has used to good effect throughout his thirty-year career in broadcasting. His comments achieved the desired response and the BBC offered its brightest star an exciting new programme: a peak-time, live, Saturday-evening show that they called *The Late, Late Breakfast Show*. By picking Noel to spearhead their all-important Saturday-night ratings battle with ITV, the BBC confirmed his position as one of the biggest stars in television.

Derek James recalls how the BBC had at first tried to get Noel to sign up for *Breakfast Time* when early-morning television was launched. Noel wasn't interested, but realised that having his name linked to breakfast TV would do him no harm. 'I would love to do it,' he told journalists.

'Certainly, getting up in the morning would be no problem after five years of doing the Radio 1 *Breakfast Show*. But nothing has been decided. I've had a lot of offers. I'd love to tackle a live chat show. I'll work for anyone who's got a good idea.'

James tells how the star held out for what he really wanted – a live Saturday-evening show. He says, 'I think Noel was very clever. He dropped *Swap Shop* at the right time and he resisted breakfast television because he thought he'd only be short-lived on air. And he's been proved right. It was very clever. I used to say to Noel, "When you do get your evening show, you'll have to call it *The Late, Late Breakfast Show*." '

But Mike Smith believes there was no way Noel would have considered breakfast television. He explains, 'I was working on *Breakfast Time* and it was always going to be current affairs. Noel would never do current affairs. There's a big gulf between current affairs and entertainment and there's a big gulf in money between them as well, certainly in the early 1980s.'

*The Late, Late Breakfast Show* was launched on 4 September 1982. Its recipe was a mixture of live satellite link-ups with celebrities around the world, and outside broadcasts. It also featured the infamous Hit Squad, in which unsuspecting members of the public became the victims of practical jokes. In the run-up to the first show, Noel admitted he had lain awake at night worrying about it. '*Swap Shop* was a very safe sort of programme but now I am accepting a challenge,' he said. 'This is like coming out of the trenches and straight into the firing line. It is a ratings war and I know that the knocking is going to come.'

He was right: the show was not a huge hit. In fact, critics were virtually unanimous in voting it a flop. Noel's right-hand girl, comedienne Leni Harper, was hurriedly dropped, and the stunts of the Hit Squad were only mildly successful. But it picked up in the second series when producer Peter Dulay, who had masterminded the *Candid*

*Camera* stunts, was signed up to help, and by the third series, when Noel was joined by Mike Smith, ratings soared.

Smith explains how he ended up as Noel's costar: 'Michael Hurll, who is one of the best TV-show directors in this country, was producing and directing *The Late, Late Breakfast Show* and he came up to me one day and asked me if I'd seen the show. I said I had and I knew it wasn't going very well. The ratings were about 4 million for its first season – and it also had a very unfortunate incident involving a car crash. They had a stunt driver in a Jensen Interceptor and this thing was jumping over some cars and it all went horribly wrong. The show nearly got taken off the air permanently as a result.

'Michael asked if I would go and do a couple of outside broadcasts for their second season. So I went and did some and the outcome of all that was they turned around and said, "You and Noel work very well together. Will you stay and do the series?" So that was it. In 1984 I started with *The Late, Late Breakfast Show*.'

Noel and Mike, who were almost as close as brothers at this period in their lives, were a dynamic partnership on air. Mike says, 'There was this unusual thing that I can never forget, and I don't know why it exists with certain broadcasters and with others it doesn't, but there was a telepathy between us. I don't want to get all grand about it, but basically we knew what we were doing before we even said it or did it, and this relationship developed on the air that was very, very funny and very charming and very warm.' Viewers loved the combination of Noel and his baby-faced sidekick, 'Smitty', and tuned in in their millions. 'We were certainly attracting a hell of an audience,' says Mike. 'I think we got about 21 million viewers. We were the only show to take *EastEnders* off the top of the charts at the time, and I remember Michael Grade, who was at that time Controller of BBC1, sent a message via Noel that he thought we were the best double act on television.'

Noel acknowledged that his and Mike's on-screen rapport

was a key factor in the show's new-found success. 'We have great mutual respect and I think he is the perfect foil to me,' he said. 'People like the anarchic side of Smitty. They're never quite sure what he's going to say next. Nor are we! He's totally outrageous.'

But, working so closely with Noel, Mike – who had always admired and liked Noel enormously – now started to notice other characteristics in his friend. He reveals, 'Noel is a natural broadcaster and a natural star and, because he's a natural star, he does have these strange sides to him which people don't understand. There is a unique thing in Noel where, when he's very successful, when it's all going very, very well, he starts to cut himself off from people. He just takes himself off into his own world and he can be seen from the outside as being a very difficult person to work with. He just goes in on himself because he's finally got total control. And once he's successful, once he's got what he wants, he's a bit like a kid in a sweet shop. He's very, very happy with himself; he doesn't need anybody else to help him out. And, really, I think one thing that goes against his personality is that he is one of those people who only really wants people around him when he needs some help.

'I didn't really mix with him that much socially when we first met because I was younger than him; he was married and I wasn't – all that stuff. But as the years went by I got to understand him better and better.'

Noel's relationship with Patricia Askew may have cost him his marriage, but it didn't last long after his divorce. Noel never mentioned her when asked about his love life, preferring instead to talk about how he was still so friendly and close to Gill. 'I am still utterly depressed and down,' he said in March 1982, while he was seeing Patricia. 'I can now understand why people want to kill themselves when their lives fall apart.' Within months, his relationship with Patricia was over for the second, and final, time.

While he had refused to publicly acknowledge Patricia as his girlfriend, Noel happily introduced his next love to the world. In early 1983, he fell for Debbie Hunter, a 23-year-old former model, and announced that she had brought him new happiness. 'She's a lovely girl, bright, beautiful and intelligent. We are more than very good friends: she's my girlfriend,' said Noel, giving Debbie the status that had been denied Patricia.

Noel, who had just been voted Third Dishiest Man on Television, behind Hollywood stars Robert Wagner and Tom Selleck, admitted he was 'completely smitten' with his new love, a beautiful blue-eyed blonde eleven years his junior. 'She's a better-looking Susan George,' he boasted. 'I met her when we were both working at a trade fair in London. I thought she looked rather nice, but I can be terribly shy at times. So I got a friend to ask her if she would have dinner with me and I'm glad to say she said yes.' But, he said, he would never walk up the aisle again. 'Although I think marriage is a marvellous institution, I don't want it. I can't imagine anything that would make me want to get married again. We are not living under the same roof but we're very happy the way things are.'

Soon after he had moved into the Manor House, Noel bought a sixty-acre farm on either side of the village to add to his land, and built up a herd of cattle. Noel's estate manager, Ray McGuirk, whose wife Hazel was the star's housekeeper, reveals how much Noel enjoyed his role as gentleman farmer. He says, 'He liked the country life. One day he was ploughing the field and was up on the tractor, dressed in all his glory with a woolly hat on. He didn't look a bit like Noel Edmonds. I can remember someone arrived and said they'd come to see Noel. I asked them which way they'd come and they said they'd driven down the main drive. I said, "In that case, you passed him. He's the man on the tractor." We also had Highland cattle with long shaggy coats, which were a showpiece. He's got a soft spot for animals, especially for his Great Danes, Toast and Honey. They were the love of his life. They were his babies.'

Noel was grateful for the loyal way in which Ray and

Hazel cared for him, and they often experienced the star's generosity. 'He really is a very generous person to work for,' says Ray. 'One year we were going to Greece on holiday and Noel came down in the middle of the afternoon to the workshop and he gave me an envelope. He told me not to open it until I was at home with Hazel, and off he went. About an hour later I went back to the Lodge House and we opened it up. There was a jokey letter saying, "I know you're going on holiday and I've made some inquiries and you can only take £20 in drachmas. That's no good to you, but perhaps you'll be able to use these." And there were $700 in the envelope, for us to take on holiday. On other occasions he would say, "You've been working hard these last few months and I've booked a table for you across at The Bell. It's all on me." The Bell at Aston Clinton is a very expensive restaurant and we'd go across there and it would all be laid on for us.'

Happily settled in the Manor House, Noel encouraged his parents to move closer to him. They left Gidea Park and bought a house in Tring in Hertfordshire, just a few miles away from Weston Turville. He had also persuaded his father to quit his job as a headmaster and work for him, filling the void left by Gill. 'He runs my business, does the VAT and handles everything for me,' said Noel. 'It is only now that he sees the books that he accepts I have got a proper job! I am thrilled about working with him. I had a happy upbringing and my parents supported me a great deal. If I can give something back, that's terrific.'

Dudley and Lydia were frequent visitors to the Manor House, and Ray recounts how he, Dudley and Noel would often spend whole days working on the estate. 'Noel wasn't like a boss at all,' he says. 'We didn't have an employer–employee relationship; we were friends. Noel would invite us up to the house in the evenings for a drink and a chat and we'd put the world to rights. Although he was in television, very rarely would he sit down and watch TV: he was more of a music man than a television man. He always had

29, Clarendon Gardens, Ilford, Essex, Noel's first home

9, Risebridge Road, Gidea Park, Essex, the house where Noel lived as a schoolboy

*Left* The Christmas card sent out by Noel's parents, when he was a 19-year-old DJ on Radio Luxembourg

*Below* Two years later, Noel gets Kenny Everett's spot on Radio 1

*Top right* The Radio 1 football team

*Bottom right* Noel celebrates as he hands over the Breakfast Show to Dave Lee Travis

*Left* Noel gets engaged to Gill Slater

*Below* Early married life

*Top right* Noel learning to drive a Formula Ford at Brands Hatch, with Gill looking on

*Bottom right* Noel and Gill outside their home, the Manor House, posing with the family cars, an E type Jaguar and a Ford GT40

A country man at heart

*Above* Noel with
girlfriend Debbie Hunter

*Left* And with current
wife Helen

*Left* Noel in Gotchaland, Bicton Park

*Below* (left to right) Stephen, Jeremy and John Taylor, who fell out with Noel over the Cricket St Thomas project

records and tapes on and he was into current affairs. He liked the radio.

'We had a very, very good relationship with him, and with his mum and dad also. If anything needed doing to the house, his dad and I would do it together. We built a proper workshop at the bottom of the garden with shelves, benches and tool racks. We eventually got round to being allowed to call Noel's mother by her Christian name. We were some of the very few people who were allowed to do so. Noel said himself, "Mum would love to be a duchess." '

Lydia, needless to say, still doted on Noel. 'She had pictures of him with the Queen and all the people he'd met,' said Ray. 'Noel bought his mum a Rolls-Royce. She wouldn't let him drive it – she said he drove too fast. I remember one day we were all there and Noel said to Hazel, "Go on, you get in the Rolls-Royce." His mum said, "Now you go careful in that!" But all he did was drive it to the bottom of the drive. Then he said to Hazel, "There you are: you're being driven in a Rolls-Royce by Noel Edmonds!" '

Ray also reveals how Noel was heartbroken when his dog Honey had to be put down: 'Danes are prone to get back-leg and back trouble and she was starting to collapse. The vet came and we had a conference about what to do and we took the vet's advice to have her put to sleep. Her quality of life wasn't as it should be and she was probably in pain as well. There was nothing they could do about it. I was the one who had to hold her while she was put to sleep. Noel didn't take it very well. The dogs were great friends of his. They knew him and they'd had great fun together. He wasn't very happy and he left me to get on with it and make a fuss of her while she was being put down.'

One of Noel's close friends during this time was Peter McMaster, a sportswear promoter whom Noel met while hosting the Radio 1 *Breakfast Show* in the 1970s. Peter explains how the two became pally after he asked Noel to promote his clothes: 'I was the sportswear manager for Slazenger and we sponsored a number of people in the sports business. I had this idea way back in the 1970s to sponsor some people in show business, and I liked Noel as a DJ and listened to him on the radio. It seemed odd that I would actually get a radio personality to wear our garments, but he was very high profile at the time. I rang the BBC, asked to speak to Noel Edmonds, and they put me through. It was one of those strange things; nowadays you couldn't do it. We used to meet at the BBC and go round the corner to the George Hotel for breakfast. We went out to dinner a couple of times and became friends. We had a similar sense of humour and we were both interested in cars.'

Peter also became friendly with Gill. 'She used to manage him and if I was delivering clothes or wanted to talk to him and he was busy I used to speak to her,' he explains. 'I suppose I was one of the few people who actually knew Gill quite well. She was a really nice girl. She did everything for him and they seemed very happy. I was surprised when they split up. I never really got to the bottom of why they did; the reason he used was children. Gill was different from Debbie. Debbie was an absolutely charming girl. She was young and vivacious; whereas Gill was more managing. Gill was the one who got everything organised when they moved into the big house. She was quite social, but much more on a one-to-one basis. She felt more comfortable with fewer people around.'

Peter recalls how Noel would hold his own private House Party at his home and challenge his friends to complete a series of feats: 'We used to go round to Noel's house for what he used to call the Manor Games. It was a big event that he'd host once a year and it would last all weekend. There'd be about twenty of us and we'd all stay over. We would split into teams and he'd test our skill over the weekend. We'd have to do things like drive a Range Rover round obstacles while blindfolded, listening to directions on a walkie-talkie. Another test was to pick up a bucket of water with a JCB and tip it into a toilet. We'd have to prepare a meal as well and take that along and then we'd get marks out of ten. There would be a big silver cup for the winner. It used to start Friday night and finish Sunday night and would be literally packed out with people. Everything was beautifully organised, with games from morning till night. They were special, fun times. Noel was a tremendous entertainer and very generous with it. He wouldn't worry about your own financial status: he invited a lot of people who came from the show-business world and were obviously very wealthy; but my wife Jan and I weren't wealthy – we just worked in the sports business. When we saw him we would either relax at his home, or he would have to fly somewhere in the helicopter and he'd take us with him for the ride. When we went to restaurants, I always tried to offer but Noel always paid. He was extremely generous.'

Peter got to know Noel extremely well during the fifteen years that they were friends. 'Noel is a very strong personality,' he explains. 'Nine times out of ten he would be the centre of attention, and I would say that he liked it – you have to in that business. He was terribly ambitious and always had lots of ideas. Every time we went round, there was a new idea that he was trying to do. He was bound to be successful because he had ideas and people to back him.'

One relationship that soured in the mid-80s was Noel's business association with Derek James. The two fell out over money, just as they had in the early 70s over the incident of the cheque. But this time it was more serious and ended up in an acrimonious row. James explains: 'I remember his father ringing me up the day after it happened and saying the two of us needed our heads banging together. He actually made Noel fly down to see me and we came to a compromise over money. But once things like that happen it's never the same again.

'I think it is something that befalls everybody eventually,' Derek says simply. 'They were good days and it is very sad when somebody forgets where they've come from and drops people when they've outlived their usefulness. I think most "personalities" are quite happy to be what they are – to be a personality or an entertainer – and leave wheeling and dealing to somebody else; but not Noel. I've never come across anybody with the make-up he's got. I don't bear him any malice – I just feel very sad the way things turned out.'

Chris Fone also disappeared from Noel's life at this point. After more than twenty years of friendship, he was simply dropped, without explanation. Chris Fone's wife, Sue, explains, 'We were in touch with Noel until his marriage broke up. I think there was a big cut-off with almost everybody from the past at that point. It was very abrupt. Everything ceased from that moment.'

Chris says sadly, 'When his first marriage went up the Swanee I lost all contact with him. We didn't fall out; I just got fed up trying to catch up with someone whom I felt wanted to make a new start.'

Mike Smith was still close to Noel, but he also thought some of his personal relationships were a bit strange. Mike, who is married to the TV presenter Sarah Greene, recalls going to stay at the house in Buckinghamshire when Noel was going out with Debbie. 'We were in his dining room and there were just the four of us – myself and Sarah, Debbie and Noel – and there was a picture on the wall. It was a very strange picture, a colour photograph taken on the lawn outside the house, of Noel posing with his cars and Gill. It was still on the wall even though he and Gill were divorced. And he pointed up at the picture and turned round to Debbie and said, in front of us, and we hardly knew Debbie, "There you are, my dear. One day that could all be yours if you behave yourself." It was the most demeaning thing you could say to anybody in other people's company.'

Despite speculative press reports that they had become engaged, all 'that' would not be Debbie's after all – whether she behaved herself or not. For Noel was about to meet Helen Soby, a woman who would steal his heart and turn his entire life upside down.

# 7 Love at First Sight

NOEL WAS SITTING on the floor of an employment agency in Maidenhead when he first saw Helen Soby. Or rather, when he first saw her ankles. 'I looked up and it got better and better,' he cooed. 'My eyes travelled upward until I got to her face and I immediately thought, Oh yes! I like you.'

It was the summer of 1985 and Noel was in the Berkshire town filming a routine with the Hit Squad for *The Late, Late Breakfast Show*. Helen, a 24-year-old former beauty queen, was the manager of the employment agency that supplied temporary secretaries for a hidden-camera sketch. Noel was completely bowled over when he saw her and wasted no time asking her out, despite the fact that he was still in a relationship with Debbie Hunter.

Noel remembers driving home 'like a little teenage love-struck boy' to change for dinner. But their relationship was almost over before it had even begun when Noel discovered that Helen had a young child. Unable to arrange for someone to look after her three-year-old daughter Charlotte for the evening, Helen left a message on his answerphone, cancelling their date. Noel was horrified. 'She stood me up because she said she couldn't get a baby-sitter,' he said. 'It was as if somebody had thrown a bucket of cold water over me. Because Helen is so attractive I was quite prepared from the moment I first saw her for the strong possibility that there might be a boyfriend, a fiancé, or even – God forbid! – a husband. Instead, I found myself confronting the one situation I hadn't bargained for. It shocked me. How could she have had a love child? It disappointed me because I had a horrid feeling I was about to fall in love with her and it was never going to come to anything because of her child.'

After stewing it over all night, Noel telephoned Helen and suggested they forget the whole thing. But he hadn't reckoned on Helen's spiritedness. 'I told her that I didn't want to go out with her, that a child wasn't in my brief,' he said. 'And she said she thought I was inviting her to dinner, not to marriage and the rest of my life, thank you very much. She said, "You found me interesting before. Why am I less interesting because I've got a daughter?" I'd never met a woman who talked that way before. She was so bullish that I liked her more and realised that it was me who was being limited.'

But their date, when Helen finally managed to get a baby-sitter, was not a success. Noel was still feeling uncomfortable about her having a child and was on his guard throughout dinner. 'I had this incredible knot in my stomach and all these thoughts flashed through my head,' he admitted. 'Could she be living with someone? Could she be married? I didn't want to get involved. I'd never seen myself falling for someone who had a child from a previous relationship. The date was a disaster because I was so secretive with her – I wouldn't tell her anything about myself and she was very unimpressed.'

Helen played it cool, which, as it turned out, was exactly the right way to play it. The fact that she didn't appear to be as keen on him as he was on her only served to heighten her attraction. He was well and truly smitten. 'I was desperate to go out with her again,' Noel confessed. 'At that time, on paper I had everything I suspect would be a lot of men's dreams – I was living in a beautiful Queen Anne manor house with a wonderful indoor swimming pool and I had an exciting lifestyle – but I wasn't happy. I became quite broody. I used to dream about a pram on the lawn and then try to visualise the woman who would be by the pram.

I'd go to work each day wondering whether today would be the day that I would meet her. Then I saw Helen. I felt she was the exact mix of person I was looking for.'

Noel and Helen were from similar backgrounds and both had teachers for parents. A ready-made family hadn't been part of Noel's dream, but what started as a highly charged sexual attraction quickly became something more serious as Noel fell head over heels in love with Helen. 'It was as if someone had walked into my life and suddenly the jigsaw fitted,' he said. 'Until Helen came along, the one magic piece was missing.' After the disastrous first date, Noel persuaded her to see him again by promising to be less secretive. He turned up for their second meeting clutching a photograph album full of pictures of his home life.

Noel was now one of the biggest names in show business and, inevitably, this new development in his private life was plastered all over the front pages of the national press. Handyman Ray McGuirk remembers the chaos that ensued when his boss first met Helen, and reveals the cat-and-mouse games the star played with reporters. 'I used to take him to meet Helen so he could dodge the press,' he says. 'I would drive him in his car and we'd meet in a hotel car park. She would come across and get in his car and I'd bring her car back to the Manor. He would ring me up to go and collect him at about midnight.'

Being thrust into the limelight was a daunting experience for Helen, who was thirteen years younger than Noel. When they gave their first interview together, Noel admitted she had found it hard at times. 'Helen has found it difficult to conduct a romance in the full glare of publicity and some of the things that have been written have upset her,' he said. 'But in many ways it has helped to bring us closer together.' He had been impressed by the cool way in which Helen had handled herself under pressure when the news of their romance got out.

She confessed she was worried that the unwelcome publicity would split them up. 'Some of the things that were said were really horrible,' she said. 'There was the suggestion that I was only interested in Noel as security for Charlotte. It makes me sound as if I'm cold and calculating and out for money, which is a really horrible idea. I don't need security that desperately. I've got a good job and I have always been proud of my independence. I never tried to hide anything from him. I told him the perfect truth about my past. I would have understood if he had been put off by all the fuss, but what it actually did was draw us closer.'

Noel also revealed that anxious friends had urged him to take his time and to make absolutely sure he knew what he was getting involved in. He also admits that, as a famous and wealthy man, he was initially worried that Helen might be a gold-digger. 'I fell for her quite quickly but I felt very vulnerable,' he says. 'I remember once I asked her what her long-term ambition was and she said "to be successful and own a nice house with quite a bit of land and breed horses". I thought, God, she's after me for my money! I tried to send her home. But she was just being very honest. My friends were worried that I wasn't prepared for the publicity our relationship would attract, but the more I thought about it the more I didn't give a damn what anybody thought. You can't really crucify somebody for having a child out of wedlock.'

Within months, love-struck Noel – who had emphatically stated that he would never walk down the aisle again – had proposed. 'I very quickly got the feeling that I couldn't do without her; that she was the one I wanted to spend the rest of my life with,' he explained. 'I really didn't think it would happen to me again – that I would meet somebody who would completely bowl me over. I was a bit resigned to having a good lifestyle and a lot of fun without ever finding that really special person who I wanted to marry. I'd had great friendships with girls but then – wallop! Suddenly I found out what it's like to really fall in love with somebody.'

This loss of control was something that didn't sit easily with Noel. He was used to being in the driver's seat with his relationships, both professional and private. But Helen Soby had managed to tilt him off his axis completely. 'It was quite frightening at first because I was on the verge of being out of control,' he admitted. 'For the first time in my life I couldn't stop thinking about somebody, to the point where I wasn't concentrating on my work. Normally I am totally committed to the job, but there were times on *The Late, Late Breakfast Show* when I knew she was in the audience and I found I couldn't keep her off my mind even while I was actually on the air.'

Friends couldn't help but notice the enormous effect that Helen had on Noel. It was as if he had been hit by a thunderbolt. His close friend Peter McMaster says, 'He appeared to be very much in love with Helen. Besotted is perhaps the right word. He fell head over heels. He couldn't believe it, and none of us could either. He'd met this girl through the TV show and next thing his life was being turned upside down. None of us in our group of friends knew Helen: she just appeared on the scene out of nowhere, and the next minute they were getting married. She came as a bit of a surprise to most of us. We didn't know about her for a while when Debbie was still around. We were all still going out for weekends together and Debbie didn't know about Helen, either.'

When Noel finally broke off his relationship with Debbie Hunter, Peter witnessed her distress at first hand. 'She was desperately upset,' he says. 'She came and stayed with me for a while to get over it. She was a very hurt girl, extremely hurt. She was very young and was obviously in love with him. Most of us were very close friends with Debbie, so we were trying to protect her and at the same time remain friends with Noel. It was very difficult because she was such a likeable girl that people tended to take her under their wing, which presumably Noel resented to some degree. These things happen and someone gets upset along the line. I know it took Debbie a long time to get over it. Noel is obviously attractive to women and clearly there are lots of women around who would have liked to go out with him because he is a famous, good-looking man, earning lots of money. But he is very single-minded and when he fell in love with Helen he got carried away on the tide. He really wanted children and Helen was the one.

'I think it was daunting for Helen because when she met Noel she went from rags to riches, really. And then to be faced with all of us, and some of the crowd being as famous as they were.' Noel's group of friends included The Who drummer Kenny Jones and Moody Blues guitarist John Lodge. 'To some degree I suppose we all looked her up and down,' Peter continues. 'She was a bit of a shock. Helen certainly didn't come from the same box of tricks as Debbie. She was very different from the sort of person we thought Noel would go out with, but she was a stunning-looking girl and she was ambitious.'

That day in the employment agency in Maidenhead was the first time that Noel saw Helen, but it was not the first time they had met. Noel loves to tell the story of how, when he was in his heyday at Radio 1, he visited Helen's local youth club to do a radio show. Helen, who was only eleven years old at the time, was not overly impressed. 'I thought you were awful – really arrogant,' she admitted to him.

At their engagement on 8 May 1986, Noel presented Helen with a glittering £10,000 diamond-and-sapphire engagement ring. 'This is the happiest day of my life,' he told reporters as he whisked his bride-to-be off on a pre-wedding holiday to the Montreux pop festival. Noel had chosen not to propose to his second wife over a romantic dinner for two, but in a packed Beverly Hills restaurant, Jimmy's, in the presence of the actor Sidney Poitier. 'She had no idea what I felt until I proposed to her in Los Angeles, when we were having dinner with the Poitiers and some other friends,' explained Noel, easily slipping into the Hollywood habit of name-dropping.

On 4 July 1986, they were married in a romantic ceremony on the shores of Loch Lomond. They had initially said they would marry on 23 July, the same day as Prince Andrew's marriage to Sarah Ferguson, so that their wedding would go unnoticed amid all the fuss over the royal wedding, but later changed their minds. Their first idea may well have been a good one, as their wedding plans inevitably leaked out. Noel was furious when scores of reporters descended on his hotel in the tiny picturesque village of Luss, setting for the TV soap opera *Take the High Road.* Noel, who delighted in springing surprises on people with his Hit Squad, was not amused when the tables were turned on him, and he called in police to clear the unwanted guests. A newspaper considered flying Charlotte's father up to disrupt the ceremony, but later thought better of it and the wedding went ahead without a hitch.

The bride and groom arrived at the village church by helicopter and were married by the Reverend Douglas Glover. Helen wore an ivory satin Victorian-style dress with a floral head-dress that matched the one worn by their bridesmaid, Charlotte. Noel's best man was his close friend Jed Hughes, who had taken over Ray McEnhill's half-share in Noel's helicopter. Noel had generously paid for the fifty guests to fly up to Scotland for the ceremony and put them up in the hotel. They were collected from Glasgow airport and ferried to the church by helicopter.

One of the guests was Peter McMaster. 'We were a bunch of very close-knit friends who had known Noel for years: Jed, Brian Aris the photographer, John Lodge, Kenny Jones and me. We were the old guard. We were all Noel's age and were very good friends and he flew us all up to his wedding. He paid for it all. He was always very generous.'

After their honeymoon, Noel and Helen returned home to Weston Turville, where they had a blessing in the picture-postcard church next to the Manor House.

Noel was naturally keen for his mother and father to like Helen, but, says Ray McGuirk, Lydia and Helen did not immediately hit it off. 'I don't think Helen got on with Noel's mother,' he says. 'I don't know if she approved of

Helen. She did make efforts to get on with her but they were a different generation completely. She was in her seventies and Helen was in her early twenties. There was a bit of a gap to try to bridge, and I think they both did what they could do to be accepted.'

Noel subsequently adopted Charlotte and he and Helen settled down to planning a family together. Falling in love, getting married and becoming an instant dad occupied the majority of Noel's time and energy in 1986, and most of the year was taken up with affairs of the heart. But, never one to let his career stand still, and feeling happier than he had done for years, Noel was on a high and believed he could achieve anything he wanted. In May, two months before his wedding, Noel set out to conquer America.

Months of negotiation had finally come to fruition and the American television network ABC commissioned five one-hour pilot shows from him. *The Noel Edmonds Show* went out at midnight coast to coast across America all week, and was pitted opposite the formidable might of US chat-show supremo Johnny Carson. Carson was the richest and single most influential figure in American television. His *Tonight* show was an American institution and successive attempts throughout the 70s and 80s to oust him from his pole position had failed. He owned his own show and, as a result, became one of the wealthiest men in the USA. Noel's audacious plan was to knock Carson from his number-one spot in the ratings and steal his crown.

Always one to do things as meticulously as possible, Noel did his homework before going on air. He hired a dialogue coach to help him to speak 'American', and spent weeks studying video tapes of Carson in action. He learnt which towns in America to mention to produce a laugh. 'Say Pittsburgh and you get roughly the same response as saying Wigan or Scunthorpe to an English audience,' he explained. Noel had dollar signs in his eyes, but insisted money wasn't his only motive. 'Initially this show is very much a gamble, but I could make millions. Johnny Carson is on tens of millions of dollars a year. The sums are so large I can't regard them with any more seriousness than the person who fills in the pools coupon and sticks it in the post,' he said. 'Of course there's a dream there at the end, but you don't think the chances of getting it are very high and you certainly don't expect the money. That's not the driving force – it would mean a lot more to me to be successful and to be the first Englishman to have cracked it on American television since David Frost in the 60s. I do like the Americans with their positive thinking. They like success and they're willing to support a trier. I'm giving this my best shot but I'm hoping I haven't bitten off more than I can chew.'

*The Noel Edmonds Show* was a zany version of *The Late, Late Breakfast Show*, with perennial favourites the Hit Squad, Golden Eggs and the Whirly Wheel Challenge. By the end of his first week the reviews were in. 'A real twit,' said the *Los Angeles Times*. 'When it comes to British humorists, Noel Edmonds is right up there with Margaret Thatcher. You might say that Noel Edmonds is taking America by calm.' 'Clumsy amateurishness,' complained the *Hollywood Reporter*. 'He dresses a bit too sharply and isn't too terribly engaging. Edmonds appears acutely aware of his strained antics.'

Noel faced a nail-biting wait while ABC decided if they wanted to sign him up for a multimillion-dollar contract. August the fifteenth was to be red-letter day. Noel had thought it all through, he said, and his plan was to commute 10,000 miles every week between Britain and America so that he could honour his contract with the BBC. It was something he was more than prepared to do.

Noel was typically gung-ho about it all, but August came and went without any announcement from the normally publicity-minded star. By September his plans had fallen through and the deal was off. Noel wasn't the first Brit to try to win over the American audience and fail, and he was philosophical about it. 'The reviews that were good were very, very good,' he said. 'The ones that were bad were very bad. But generally the show went down well. We got very good audience figures but it went out at midnight, which is hardly the best slot for it. I don't think I did too badly. I had five nights to win over America and Carson has had 25 years to get it right.' He claimed to have turned down a £1 million contract because he couldn't bear to be parted from Helen and announced that, for the first time in his life, his career now came second. 'I decided that family life was much more important than going off to the States,' he said. 'When you've only been married eight weeks you don't want to be apart from each other.'

He would return to the States in the spring of 1987, he revealed, to film a series of teatime shows. The following month, Noel joyfully announced that Helen was pregnant with their first child, and threw into doubt whether he would now seek work in America at all. He said, 'I think the baby will influence my plans – the baby is more important than America.'

But while his dabble in US TV may not have been as successful as he had hoped, it did teach him probably the single most significant lesson of his entire career – the importance of owning the format to his shows. This knowledge would later cement his power base in the industry and make him one of the top earners in British TV.

By the time that 1986 was drawing to a close, Noel had never felt more contented. He had a thriving helicopter-chartering business based at Battersea Heliport in London, and was looking forward to spending his first Christmas as a family with Helen and Charlotte. He was also delighted about the baby Helen was expecting. 'I can't imagine ever being happier,' he enthused.

But his words must have tempted fate. Disaster was looming just round the corner. A tragic accident was about to rob a young man of his life and send Noel's career into a nose dive. The fallout from this would last for years and haunt Noel for the rest of his life.

The bubble was about to burst.

# 8 The Bubble Bursts

THE DEATH OF Michael Lush, a contestant on *The Late, Late Breakfast Show*, was a tragedy that shocked Britain and rocked Noel's career to its foundations. Michael, a 25-year-old self-employed builder, plunged 120 feet to his death after a stunt he was rehearsing for the show went horribly wrong. Just hours before the fatal accident on 13 November 1986, he had talked enthusiastically about his shot at fame and spoke of the faith he had in the BBC. 'I am not scared because if it wasn't safe they wouldn't do it,' he said trustingly.

Michael, who had a love of daredevil sports, was excited about his 'adventure of a lifetime' as a Whirly Wheel competitor on the hugely successful show. 'I deliberately asked to do something which would look good and be a bit more dangerous than the usual,' he said. 'I would have been happy to do anything as long as it didn't involve water, as I can't swim.' He admitted that his fiancée, Alison Toop, who was two days away from her 23rd birthday, was nervous about the stunt, and he joked that it would be his birthday present to her. 'She has even refused to watch me train and will just turn up for the show,' he said. 'It is funny because it was her idea I go in for it.'

But within 24 hours of giving the interview Michael was dead. He fell from an 'exploding' crate suspended from a crane when his bungee rope failed. Alison and his mother Vera had both been assured by the BBC that there would be no risk to Michael whatsoever, but within hours it was blatantly obvious that someone somewhere had messed up on an alarming scale. A shocking catalogue of errors was revealed as police and safety experts began to investigate the accident. It transpired that no safety officer was present for the stunt; the stunt was new yet it was tried on an untrained member of the public; the expert hired by the BBC was not a stunt man; and no provision, such as a safety wire, was made in case Michael Lush fell out of the crate before it reached its full height. The gate-type carabiner clip used to attach the rope to the crate could have snapped open, due to the rubbing action of the rope. A screw-in clip may have been safer, and, whatever clip was used, there should have been two for extra safety, as well as two ropes for the same reason. The Dangerous Sports Club was not consulted, and said that, if it had been, it would have insisted that one of its members went up in the crate with Michael.

The BBC broke the terrible news of her son's death to fifty-year-old Vera Lush in a telephone call, without waiting for the police to tell her the news in person. Bewildered Mrs Lush at first thought the call was a cruel hoax and phoned her neighbour, Edwin Rawlings, who raced round to the house and found her collapsed on the floor in a state of shock. Mr Rawlings telephoned the BBC to see if the call had been genuine, and it took 45 minutes before they rang back and confirmed the shattering news. Police said they were 'utterly appalled, shocked and dismayed' at the way the BBC bungled the call to Mrs Lush, and insisted that they should have been called first so that they could break the news to her properly.

The way Vera Lush heard of her son's death was indicative of the panic and confusion at the BBC in the hours and days that followed the tragedy. Mike Smith, Noel's copresenter on *The Late, Late Breakfast Show*, was in the thick of it all and well remembers the chaos that ensued: 'Neither Noel nor I was there when it happened, but I was very much on the spot because I was recording a kids' TV show at Television Centre the afternoon that Michael Lush was killed. He was killed out in Oxfordshire but obviously the word got back and I was called into the boss's office to try to sort out what they should do. They were running around like the proverbial headless chickens, with no idea what to do. It was a big, big shock – a complete bolt from the blue. I said, "The first thing to do is get hold of Noel and we'll speak to him." The press was already on to it and was trying to get quotes. There weren't that many mobile phones around and it was very difficult for us to make a network of communication over the whole thing to keep it tightened down until we knew the facts.'

That night, Thursday, reporters and photographers converged on Mike Smith's London home. While they waited outside for a comment from the star, Mike was inside on the telephone to Noel, persuading him that they should visit Michael's relatives. He explains: 'Because I lived in London and Noel didn't, I was getting all the doorstepping that night and he wasn't. I spoke to him on the phone and said, "Look, we must go and see the family. We can do this without commotion. We don't need the press involved: they won't follow me – I'll shake them off. It will be fine, but we must see that family and we must talk to them to show that we care about what's happened." '

Michael Lush's body was taken to Stoke Mandeville Hospital near Aylesbury, just up the road from where Noel lived. Mike says, 'I drove out to Weston Turville and met Noel at his house on the Friday morning and we went to the hospital. The family had been to the morgue and we met them privately afterwards. I'd insisted on that. We met up with them and it was fine. There were some other people there as well as his mother and his fiancée Alison. It was tough but it had to be done – you can't shirk away from these things. And I sensed in Noel that there was no way he really wanted to confront this. But you have to confront it.'

Later that afternoon, Noel and Mike were called in to see Bill Cotton, the man who had helped to make Noel a star. Bill, who had risen to the lofty height of Managing Director of BBC Television, gave them the unsurprising news that that week's show had been cancelled. 'We were told, "The show is off the air this week obviously, but let's meet up on Monday. Let's replan the series without stunts, and let's get back on the air as soon as possible," ' says Mike.

Talking to reporters outside his house about the 'worst night of my life', Noel said, 'I cried a lot last night. Inevitably people are wise after the event, but I bear a lot of the responsibility. It's my show. I'm not the sort of insensitive person who can say, "That's show business." '

No one could believe what had happened. A show that had built its reputation on laughs and fun had just been responsible for the death of one of its viewers. Just over a month before, Noel had confidently talked about the Whirly Wheel stunts and had been quick to play down the danger element. 'This is not snuff TV and we're not in the game of putting anyone through any unnecessary risk,' he promised. 'Every precaution is taken to ensure that nobody comes to any harm. But at the same time there has to be an element of real daring.'

Now his words had come back to haunt him.

Vera Lush was too distraught to say much. Her only words in the days immediately following her son's death were, 'I feel very bitter. Somebody has to pay for this. I just want to be left alone to cry with my family.'

Three days after Michael Lush's death, Noel sat down for an exclusive interview with a trusted journalist. He and Helen posed for photographs as he told how he had decided to quit the show. 'Believe it or not, it was one of the simplest decisions I have made,' he said. 'There was no way I could go on. After a second sleepless night, Helen and I talked it over on Saturday morning and, like a lot of decisions that come from the heart, it was very uncomplicated. I went to the BBC with Helen to see Bill Cotton, feeling a degree of relief because there was absolutely no doubt in my mind that I was doing the right thing. There had been talk at first of carrying on, but then I began to think to myself, There is no way I can walk down those steps on Saturday. Then I suddenly realised that, if I was honest with myself, I couldn't imagine walking down those steps ever again.'

From his initial feeling that the show could survive the tragedy, Bill Cotton was also forced to rethink his decision when he saw the Saturday-morning papers. A barrage of criticism was directed at the BBC and it was announced that it could face prosecution over Michael Lush's death. A team of investigators from the Health and Safety Executive was at the scene of the accident in Long Crendon, Buckinghamshire, and said it could take legal action against the BBC if necessary. It also revealed that its officers in Bradford had prevented *The Late, Late Breakfast Show* from carrying out a stunt two weeks before when a volunteer was to be plucked by helicopter from the top of a chimney stack seconds before it was detonated.

The spokesman said, 'We told them that if they insisted on going ahead with the stunt we would serve them with an enforcement notice. It was a very dangerous thing to attempt. On Mr Lush's death, we do have the power to take legal action once we know what went wrong.'

*The Late, Late Breakfast Show*'s reputation was further damaged when top stunt man Jim Dowdall said he had refused to help in stunts for the show because they weren't allowing enough practice time. He said, 'They asked me to advise on the famous stagecoach-jumping trick. I said it would take a long time to get it right. I was told I had just one week to rehearse it and I said it would be impossible to do it properly and I wanted nothing to do with it.'

The actors' union, Equity, said it was planning to complain to the BBC about the increasing use of members of the public in programmes. It said, 'We deeply regret this has happened but it is a reflection of the growing tendency to use ordinary members of the public for this kind of entertainment.'

Secretary Barbara Sleeman, a former competitor on the show, said that she had broken her shoulder three years before when she was blasted out of a cannon on the programme after only one hour's tuition.

And Hampshire police said they had officially complained to the BBC about the way it handled breaking the news to Mrs Lush.

Mike reveals: 'On Saturday morning, less than 24 hours after we were told the show would go on, the newspapers were published and Bill Cotton had them all in his office. He just turned round and said, "We can't bring this series back. The press has killed it. It's dead. It's gone." ' According to Mike, Bill Cotton was adamant that neither Noel nor Mike, nor anyone else connected to the show, should speak to the newspapers about what had happened. Mike says, 'A statement was sent round from Bill Cotton to both Noel and I saying, "This is the decision that I have reached and we are all in full agreement that nobody talks to the press." And so I didn't talk to the press. But Noel went straight out, leant over his garden gate and blubbed. He said, "Oh, this is the end of me. I can't go back on television." '

Noel's decision to disobey his boss's orders shocked Mike Smith and he began to suspect that, now the heat was on, as far as Noel was concerned it was each man for himself. 'I don't really know what the future holds,' Noel said. 'Bill Cotton has been fantastic and has told me that when I feel ready we will talk through some new ideas. But this has knocked me sideways. It's a funny feeling when the motivation for something is completely knocked out of you. I feel like the racing driver who gets out of his car for good saying that it has stopped being fun. That worries me. At the moment I just don't want to do it any more because the wrong emotions are inside me. I am not being dramatic and saying that I am going to quit public life, but I think that, in terms of working out what I want to do from now on with my career, I have to decide whether this kind of pressure and responsibility is what I really want for my own personal happiness. At the moment the horizon is not bleak – it's just not in focus. But I am not feeling sorry for myself. I feel 100 per cent better for having made the decision.

'What I do next will largely depend on public reaction to the tragedy. My success has been very much based on the nature of my relationship with the public. Through everything that I have done, there has been the constant theme of a good rapport with audiences. I don't know whether what has happened has damaged that rapport, although I fear that it may have affected my credibility as the sort of nice guy who comes on the telly having fun and being seen to have fun. So far I have had a lot of nice reactions from the BBC and local people, who have put notes through the letter box.'

Talking about the accident, he said, 'Most of the stunts were illusions. There had to be an element of daring, but not of real danger, and there is a lot of difference between those two things. If I had had the slightest doubt about the safety aspect then I would have requested that the Whirly Wheel was dropped from the show. If there was only a million-to-one chance of something going wrong, that would have been unacceptable. In that sense – even though I personally had nothing to do with choosing the stunts, selecting the people who took part, or presenting that section of the show – the very fact that I never asked for it to be dropped means that I must take some of the responsibility. I haven't done anything to be ashamed of and I don't envisage that I shall be shunned. There will still be plenty of things to do and hopefully there will still be companies who will be happy to have my name associated with them.'

After ten of the happiest months of his life, Noel was understandably worried that he might be facing a bleak future. He had the responsibility of a wife and stepdaughter and a baby on the way. His life had looked so rosy, but in a few seconds everything had changed. For the second time in five years, he seriously worried that he might lose his beloved Manor House. 'It's so sad going through the diary and crossing out all the Fridays and Saturdays that would have been taken up with *The Late, Late Breakfast Show*,' he said. 'It's a funny feeling to find that I suddenly have nothing to do when 80 per cent of the next eighteen months had been mapped out for me. Suddenly it's all gone. I talked through everything with Helen, and together we are having to reassess our long-term future and rethink the financial aspect. The bottom line is that we might have to sell the house – although hopefully it won't come to that. It would break my heart if I had to get rid of this place. It represents everything I have worked for over the years.'

Although *The Late, Late Breakfast Show* had been axed only the day before, Noel, ever the pragmatist, revealed that he had already given a lot of thought to his next move. 'There are certain safe things careerwise that I could do in television, but I wouldn't get any personal satisfaction from that, and I don't want to go back to being a presenter of other people's fodder,' he insisted. 'I would need a show that I could put my own stamp on. I like the excitement of live television. There are few things I would crow about, but I do believe that in a live studio situation I can hold my own with the best of them. But at the moment I can't see what other openings exist for me in live television. I know I will get itchy feet, but I think I have to be patient and hope that the right thing will come up.' He even managed to look on the bright side: 'You never know, perhaps this will give me the stepping stone I need to get into more adult entertainment,' he said.

But in the event, Noel was not off air for long. He returned to the nation's television screens seven weeks later for *The Late, Late Breakfast Show*'s traditional Christmas Day programme. But that year it was to be different. For one thing it would be called *Christmas Morning With Noel*; and secondly, his costar Mike Smith would not be live on air with him.

Mike tells how he began to realise that Noel was edging him out: 'We always did a Christmas-morning special which wasn't called *The Late, Late Breakfast Show*, but it was him and I doing stuff. I was always out and about in a helicopter flying all over the countryside delivering presents and doing live link-ups back into the show. That year the BBC said they wanted to do a Christmas special and get it back on the air and asked if I would be a part of it. I said, "Sure," but then I realised that everything I was going to do for the show was on film. I said, "Why am I not doing it live? Why am I not with Noel?" and I was told, "Oh, well Noel thinks that would just revive too many memories of the old show." I said Noel hadn't spoken to me about it, and they said, "No, but that's what he feels." So I was confined to film for it.'

Mike felt let down by Noel and claims that after Christmas, when he began to experience contractual problems with the BBC, Noel – his friend for thirteen years – simply abandoned him. 'After Christmas, when I still had three months of my contract left to run, the BBC tried to stop paying me,' Mike explains. 'There was a big fight going on between them and my agent, and Noel just ran for cover. Those are, for me, defining moments of what he's like. He certainly deserted me over the whole *Late, Late Breakfast Show* thing. I couldn't believe what he did.'

Mike found Noel's betrayal of him particularly hard to take because of the nature of their friendship. It wasn't as if he felt he had been let down by just anybody: it had been Noel who inspired Mike to become a disc jockey and, later, follow in his footsteps into TV. Mike had always liked and respected him and was the closest thing to a brother that Noel had ever had. Now he saw a side to the star that he had only glimpsed before. He explains: 'Noel is this strange character, a bit Jekyll and Hyde. When things are going great, he's a really nice person to be around. But when he's on a downer, when the ratings are dropping and people are pointing fingers, he can get very nasty and very defensive. That was the last I heard from Noel until I fell out of the sky two years later.'

In effect it was the end of their friendship. In 1988, Mike and his wife Sarah Greene were involved in a serious helicopter accident. The couple were flying from High

Wycombe in Buckinghamshire to the West Country on a Saturday afternoon and were about to land when their tiny bubble helicopter crashed into trees. They were lucky to survive but were badly injured and were taken to Cheltenham Hospital. The accident was a major news story and the press was camped outside the hospital, eager for any news on the couple's progress. Mike was pleased and surprised to hear from his old friend. He says, 'Noel rang the hospital about five or six days after the accident and left a message for me. I rang him back and he said, "Oh, I really want to come and see you and Sarah at the hospital." I said, "We're not in a very good state, but sure – drop in, come and see us." '

'After he came to the hospital I didn't really see him again. I did try to see him one Saturday morning when he was doing *House Party*. There was a story about to break in the press, something to do with the Michael Lush thing. I can't remember what it was – it was years later – but the press was all over us and I went in to see him to say, "I'm not saying anything and I'm sure you're not," but I couldn't get near him. He was being heavily defended by his producer Michael Leggo, and he wouldn't see me.' It was a sorry end to a once great friendship. Just like Chris Fone, Derek James, and others before him, Mike was left out in the cold and wondering what he had done to fall foul of his friend.

The period immediately following Michael Lush's death was a grim one for Noel and he became more guarded than before. The tragedy marked the beginning of a more private Noel, one who increasingly withdrew into a tight inner sanctum of family and a few close friends. He cast off his old, pre-Helen life, and many of the people who went with it. He found that having Helen to talk things over with was all he needed. As a new husband and father, he felt he had a duty to Helen to be successful, and when his show was axed so unexpectedly he felt that he'd let her down bitterly. But in a good marriage adversity pulls a couple together, and that is what Noel was lucky enough to find with Helen.

In an interview on Christmas Eve, he paid tribute to his wife. 'The past few weeks have been for me a period of quiet reflection,' he said. 'I have been under a tremendous amount of pressure. For the first time in my life I had two and a half other people in my life to consider – the half being the baby we are expecting in May. I really wondered whether I wanted to be a public figure on TV any longer. I talked it over with Helen and it was invaluable to have her advice as she is someone outside show business. I have only known Helen eighteen months but because of what has happened I feel as though we have been married for eighteen years – I mean that in the nicest possible way.'

He admitted he had been worried how his fans would react to his going back on TV, but in the end, he said, it had been they who had persuaded him to go on. 'What swayed me was the reaction of the public. The BBC has logged thousands of letters from people giving me their support.' One of those letters was from his old friend Paul Burnett.

Paul reveals: 'I remember writing to him after that dreadful incident with Michael Lush and later on I saw him at Dave Lee Travis's house. He was fairly philosophical about it. The trouble with the BBC is that it has such an eminence that if you were going to do a stunt like that you would assume that it was OK because it's got the BBC stamp on it. But it turned out that the guy who had set the stunt up wasn't qualified. Noel was badly let down there, I think, and he just felt desperately sorry. I know he was very upset but I don't think it was any sort of a setback in the career thing.'

Noel said any lingering doubts melted away when he went to record the Christmas special of his BBC quiz *Telly Addicts* and the audience gave him a five-minute standing ovation which left him close to tears. One fan in particular had missed seeing him on the box – four-year-old Charlotte. 'She has been very upset that I have not been on the telly,' said Noel. 'She has been very disappointed. Obviously she has very little idea of what has occurred, but she kept asking when I was going to appear. It was a question I simply couldn't answer. She has been very proud to see her daddy on TV and of course I want to make her happy.'

In one of the many interviews he did in the weeks following the accident, Noel said he believed the young man's death would haunt him for the rest of his life. 'The memory of this dreadful accident will always be with me and will influence everything I do in television,' he said. But in another interview he claimed he was not 'devastated' by the death. 'What happened was a great shock to everybody, but "devastated" means I was out of control. I wasn't. It caused a period of reflection. Everyone has realised that this has been a difficult period for me and it was a terrible thing to have happened.'

When he appeared on the Terry Wogan show he claimed he had been plagued with death threats following the accident. He told how 'nutters' had called at his home and threatened him, and that Helen had also been terrorised. 'We had nutters at the house, and I mean that in the true sense of the word,' he said, adding that he had been forced to ask for police protection. *The Late, Late Breakfast Show*'s producer, Michael Hurll, was also the victim of a massive hate campaign. It was an unnerving time for the Edmonds family and it didn't seem likely that the new year would be any better.

In January, the inquest into Michael Lush's death was held, focusing the spotlight back on Noel once again. As the jury unanimously recorded a verdict of misadventure, Michael's mother Vera sat quietly weeping. Noel did not attend.

Coroner Rodney Corner warned the BBC that it should never again allow such a stunt to go ahead without a safety officer being present. 'I am sure the BBC will take the lesson to heart,' he said. 'The BBC must closely examine the wisdom of using stunts such as we have heard described in this case, where it was fraught with danger from the moment the box ascended into the air with Michael Lush inside.'

It was revealed that the BBC had paid Mrs Lush £120,000 compensation. A statement from her solicitor, Robin Wintle, said, 'Before Michael was taken to rehearse the stunt, his mother and his girlfriend Alison Toop were reassured by the BBC that the best experts and a stunt man were in charge, and, although the stunt was to look dangerous, there was, in fact, to be no risk at all. The evidence as it emerged has obviously distressed and deeply upset both of them. They are amazed that the first and last person to test the equipment live was Michael. The expert hired to supervise the stunt was no expert at all, and he and those in control ignored the advice given by all persons who did have the relevant experience.' And it ended, damningly: 'Money will not compensate for the loss of Michael.'

Afterwards, Mrs Lush said bravely, 'I have obviously had a lot of pain and suffering and will continue to have a lot of pain and suffering for a long time, but gradually I shall pick up the pieces and get on with my life.' Michael's fiancée Alison said she thought the jury should have ruled that Michael died through lack of care. She said tearfully, 'I am appalled and disgusted at the verdict. I'd like to see a change in the law to allow proceedings to be brought.' She said she was not satisfied with the explanation of the accident given by BBC production manager David Nicholson and stunt adviser Paul Matthews. 'I certainly do not think they should have ignored the advice of experts,' she said. 'I do not feel that Mr Matthews was qualified in any way whatsoever to do what he did, and I think David Nicholson should have found somebody with a lot more experience.' And she criticised Noel for not attending the inquest even though it was held only thirty miles from his home.

Noel also came into criticism from other quarters, most notably from the legendary Fleet Street columnist Jean Rook. 'Innocent as Edmonds was of the stunt setup, not everyone saw him in the best TV lighting directly after the inquest on Lush, which he didn't attend,' she wrote. 'I had begun this interview sympathetic to Mr Edmonds. He had

had TV history's most ghastly break. As a *Swap Shop* fanatic, I'd come here deliberately loving him, and aggressively on his side. Now it was all going wrong. Again. I was stunned by his smugness ... Nearly every journalist but me has labelled him as a pushy little opportunist with a concrete conscience ... Mr Edmonds, by now, struck me as chillingly ambitious as a Habitat ice box. Where was his feeling for Mr Lush's bereaved family, and his hot, non-crocodile tears?'

A somewhat stilted statement, issued on Noel's behalf after the inquest, said, 'Although Mr Edmonds did not know Mr Lush and wasn't involved in any way with his death, he was of course the host of the TV programme in which Mr Lush was taking part. There is no verdict which could have changed Mr Edmonds' feelings of deepest sympathy with the Lush family for all which has occurred.'

But when told of Alison Toop's comments, the star took steps to defend himself and his words showed all too clearly that the criticisms had hurt. He said, 'All the officials concerned with the inquest recognised that I was in no way involved with the accident, otherwise I would have been called. Indeed, I was advised that my presence could actually be a hindrance to the proceedings, by diverting attention from the main issue and making it appear that I sought personal publicity. I expressed my sincere and profound grief over the tragedy and some accused me of shedding too many tears. Throughout this whole tragedy I have been used as a general whipping post. I have been in a no-win situation. However, my consolation is the certain knowledge that at all times I have acted correctly and with sincerity. If others still wish to criticise me, then I have to be philosophical and say that such is the price of fame.'

Throughout this unhappy period, Noel virtually shut himself away in the seclusion of the Manor House to lick his wounds. There he had everything that he needed: Helen and Charlotte; his parents, who were there most days; and a helicopter so he could get in and out without having to see anyone. Nigel McKinnon-Clark, landlord of the local pub, The Chequers, recalls how Noel had once been a regular customer but was seen less and less in the village during that troubled time. 'Noel was quite good fun when he was living in Weston Turville,' he says. 'He used to come into the pub fairly regularly, normally twice a week. He was always good fun to talk to. He didn't exactly mix with everybody – he'd come in and get a table where his back was to the main bar area so nobody would notice him – but my wife and I were quite friendly with him and we went out to dinner with him a few times. But there was a period of time when he had a lot of problems, not least the fact that a chap had been killed and his show was shut down. There were fairly major problems and he actually didn't work for about six months. He didn't talk about it at all; in fact he very much stayed at home for quite some time.'

In March, Noel faced more worry when Helen, who was seven and a half months pregnant, was rushed to hospital with serious internal bleeding. When she was allowed home she was confined to bed on doctor's orders. 'It's been a terrific strain,' Noel admitted. 'We are keeping our fingers crossed.' As a first-time father-to-be, Noel was understandably anxious. 'She had a lot of bad pain, which is a bit worrying, particularly for me, because it is the first time I've been down this road. It is just one of those things. There is no danger she will lose the baby. It is just a question of lying down and having a good rest. It is a shame because everything was going along very well.'

Noel said he had turned down the chance to make a version of *The Late, Late Breakfast Show* for Channel 10 in Australia because he didn't want to miss seeing his baby being born. 'There is no way I will miss the birth,' he said. 'I can't wait. It will be the best day of my life.'

Lorna Edmonds came into the world on 12 May 1987, bringing some much needed joy into Noel's life. She kept her mother and father waiting for four days before weighing in at 7lb 14oz at the Royal Buckinghamshire Hospital in Aylesbury. Noel was ecstatic. 'It was an incredible experience,' he gushed. 'It was so special. I've wanted to be a father for a very long time – but the wait was worth it. I just feel brilliant. Lorna is so beautiful.' And he added, 'I'm exhausted myself so God knows how Helen feels – she had to do all the hard work!'

One of the first people to see the new baby Edmonds was Noel's handyman, Ray McGuirk. He recalls the scene at Helen's hospital bedside just hours after she had given birth: 'We had a great time at the hospital. I was the first person to see her outside of her mother and Noel, who went to see Helen on the day that Lorna was born. Helen had an urge for a Big Mac so Noel sent me into Aylesbury to McDonald's. I asked him how many he wanted and he said, "Bring us a dozen back." So he gave them all to the nurses and then he sent me for a case of champagne and everyone was drinking champers.'

Noel was so happy he wanted the whole world to know. When Helen returned home from hospital with Lorna, he paid £350 for a plane to circle above the Manor House trailing a banner saying, 'CONGRATULATIONS, HELEN. LOVE YA, NOEL.' He also spent £1,200 filling their home with flowers. Like all new fathers, within days he admitted he had already forgotten what it was like to have a good night's sleep: 'I'm knackered. I didn't get much sleep in the days leading up to the birth because I was so nervous. And I have hardly had any at all since Lorna came home. It's just as well I'm not working on TV regularly at the moment because the make-up team would be working overtime. The trouble is, Lorna is as good as gold all day but can't settle at night. And, like most fathers I suppose, I'm overanxious about her. She only has to snuffle in her sleep and I'm sitting bolt upright, wide awake.'

Lorna's birth had made Dudley and Lydia grandparents at last, and Noel was touched to see how happy they were. He said, 'I think they had both given up hope of ever becoming grandparents. They tried hard not to be emotional, but when I collected them and drove them to the hospital Dad was in tears before we had even left the house. And when we gathered round the bed, with Helen clutching this gorgeous little bundle, all three Edmonds were bawling their eyes out. And we had another good cry together when we got home.'

Television presenter John Craven, one of Noel's best friends, was asked to be godfather.

Lorna had thick dark hair, like her mum, but Helen said everyone agreed that the baby looked exactly like Noel. 'She's definitely got his nose,' she said fondly. Noel admitted he was still somewhat dazed by the dramas and upheavals of the previous twelve months, a period he described as 'a mixture of dreams and nightmares'. But it was clear that Lorna's arrival had done him the world of good. He said, 'I do sometimes wonder how I would have got on if Helen hadn't been around. That was so important to me because there was a base to fall back on emotionally. I'd got the solidarity which I didn't have a year before. I'm feeling very positive about things now. It's no good being pathetic and feeling sorry for yourself. You never know where the next thump is coming from, and if you live your professional life in the fast lane those thumps are going to come at you more quickly. You have to be philosophical. It's the old thing about getting out of the kitchen if you can't stand the heat. But it does help if you've got someone standing next to you in the kitchen.'

He also talked about his plans to adopt Charlotte. 'Charlotte is as much my daughter as Lorna, and I hope to adopt her as soon as possible,' he said. 'I'm determined not to have a favourite. Being Dad to her for over a year has taught me patience and understanding. We never pressured her into calling me Daddy, so I was over the moon when she started of her own accord.'

Noel had done his best to put the trauma of the accident behind him and by September 1987, ten months after Michael Lush's death, he had clearly had enough of people mentioning it. In an astonishing interview with the *Daily Mirror*, he said, 'The accident is so boring I can't bring myself to talk about it any more. I'm sure the public are sick and tired of it. I've come to terms with it now. I'll never forget it, but it doesn't haunt me. Before the accident I used to be known as "Zany Noel Edmonds". Now I'm "Devastated television star" and all that. Well, I'm not devastated and, though I will never forget and never wish to be involved in that form of broadcasting again, I don't think anything is served by me going on about it.'

He went on to plug his new 'comeback' show, the BBC family game *Whatever Next?*, which he had devised himself, and admitted he was glad to be back on air. 'I have missed being on TV enormously,' he said. 'I never thought I would, but I have felt deeply that something was missing.' The new show was a logical extension of *The Late, Late Breakfast Show*, he said. 'It's about the fact that people seem to enjoy doing amusing and unusual things if you point a television camera at them. Although the show is done in the studio, we filmed quite a lot in the street and we are proving the principle that everybody can be famous for fifteen minutes. It's astounding what people will do for little Noel on the telly.'

Needless to say, there would be no stunts involved. 'We had a classic case of paranoia at the start of filming the new series when one of the contestants mentioned she did parachuting,' he said. 'Everyone's immediate reaction was, "God, no, anything to do with jumping, dropping down – horrendous!" until we pulled ourselves together and realised we were being ridiculous.'

Noel's career appeared to be back on track. He had negotiated a new four-year contract with the BBC estimated at £1 million. And he had not forgotten what he had learnt in America: the new deal gave him a great deal of control over the show through his newly created production company, Unique Television, part of the Unique Group set up by the star in 1986. 'It's the first time, I think, that the

BBC has licensed an idea off a presenter,' he said proudly. 'But I'm only involved in the creative side, not the production.' His outside interests were also blossoming: his helicopter-chartering company was doing well and he signed a three-year promotion contract with the sportswear company Adidas which would involve him painting his helicopters in their colours.

By October 1987, back on air, and with his future career once more looking assured, Noel relaxed and felt he could get back to normal.

But Noel's TV 'comeback' was not a success. *Whatever Next?* was panned by critics and sent up on the satirical TV show *Spitting Image*. They ran a sketch which implied he had taken *A Question of Sport*'s What Happens Next? round and turned it into a whole show. Saying that he didn't want to do another series, Noel said, 'I simply believe I can do better than that.' *Whatever Next?* and Noel's other main BBC show, *Telly Addicts*, were both recorded in advance and the star said he was itching to get back to live television. 'There is nothing quite like the excitement of doing a live show in front of an audience,' he said. He had his eye on the prime-time slot opposite Cilla Black's *Blind Date*. He said, 'Taking on *Blind Date* would be a real challenge.'

He would, of course, get the chance to do just that, but not for another four years. In the meantime, Helen had a few plans of her own up her sleeve. Noel's life was set to change yet again.

# 9 A Fresh Start

NOEL ADORED THE Manor House. 'I love this house and the only way they'll move me from here is when they carry me out in a box,' he was fond of saying. 'My great dream is that there will still be an Edmonds living here in a hundred years' time.' It was unthinkable to those who knew him that Noel would ever leave his beloved Manor willingly. But Helen had other ideas.

Like many second wives, Helen objected to living in a house that held so many memories of her husband's life before he met her. Everywhere she looked, she was confronted with the past. Even in the bedroom she woke up to furnishings that her predecessor, Gill, had chosen. She told Noel she wanted to move and, to everyone's surprise, Noel eventually agreed. For if there was anything that he loved more than his house, it was making his wife happy. He couldn't find it in him to refuse her anything. Former neighbour Nigel McKinnon-Clark reveals how Noel was putty in his wife's hands. 'Helen is a very strong-willed woman,' he explains. 'She knows what she wants and she usually gets it. I think he just melts, really. She's a pretty sexy woman and she does dress in a sexy way. He's only got eyes for her. She was the instigator of them moving away. She thought it was his house and she wanted to have *their* house.'

The Manor House was surrounded by beautiful open countryside, but Noel had felt uneasy for some time about the fact that the village was being encroached upon by bulldozers as the commuter belt widened. The house had soared in value in the years that Noel had owned it, and he realised that for the same amount of money he could afford to buy an enormous estate in the country. With the luxury of his own private helicopter, he was lucky enough to be able to live almost anywhere and still be able to work in London. While his neighbours faced journeys of up to ninety minutes each way if they worked in town, Noel could fly hundreds of miles in the same time. Helen wanted a lot of land so that she could indulge her love of horses, and the more he thought about it the more Noel fancied the prospect of life as a country squire.

The Manor House was put on the market in June 1988. Noel had paid £100,000 for it ten years before, but estate agents now valued it at £1.5 million. Noel had added a luxury leisure complex on to the house and that boosted the price. He had spent £250,000 on an indoor swimming pool, gym, sauna, solarium and Jacuzzi. But, in the event, the house went for £200,000 more than the asking price. Noel agreed a deal with a local builder for £1.7 million and the new buyer said that Noel and Helen could stay on in the house until they found somewhere else to live. This was just as well: selling the house had been easy; finding another one wasn't. They spent endless weeks fruitlessly searching for the right property. They had set their heart on the West Country, where Helen had family, and they wanted somewhere completely unspoilt and private, with lots of land.

In the autumn they found just such a place. Broomford Manor, a Victorian pile in the heart of Devon, was set in 855 acres of land and came complete with its own herd of wild deer. Noel and Helen thought it would be the perfect place to raise their family. The 36-roomed house, built in 1871, nestled on the edge of Dartmoor and looked out on to open farmland. It had fifteen bedrooms, a huge drawing room, music room, several studies, gun rooms and three bathrooms. There was also a massive stable block for Helen's horses, a tack room and a separate coach house. The grounds encompassed three farms, a formal garden, kitchen garden, acres of woodlands and the River Okement, which meandered through the estate. It all added up to one word: perfection.

But the Edmonds faced a nail-biting battle to buy the property because it was being sold in seven separate lots. 'When we first saw the estate we fell in love with it,' Noel said. 'We knew straight away it was a bit of a gem. I found out about it in September and we had quite a struggle to get it. More than 25 people bid for it. Some were developers who wanted to asset-strip the estate. It was sold by sealed bids in seven lots and we had to buy all of them. It was nerve-racking.' Noel had to make sure that he topped everyone else's bids and he managed to secure all seven lots by paying a rumoured £800,000 over the asking price. The estate had been expected to go for £1.7 million and he paid closer to £2.5 million. But, as far as Noel was concerned, it was money well spent. He also splashed out £94,000 on a Bentley Turbo car to complete his new lord-of-the-manor image.

Life as a country squire promised to be a placid affair, which was exactly what Noel wanted. His nearest neighbours were the inhabitants of Jacobstowe, a tiny hamlet with 200 people and no pub, post office or shops. 'I hope this move will change my lifestyle,' said Noel, happily. 'I will organise my life so I can spend a lot of time here and use my helicopter to get to work. I want to get my act together so we can enjoy what we have bought. Previously, the temptation to keep working, even on my days off, has been irresistible, but I hope the move to Devon will make a sort of psychological break for me. We love the people and countryside and we are hoping it will be a lovely place to bring up our family.' There seemed to be no regrets at leaving the Manor House.

He would fly himself the 210 miles to work at the BBC

studios in London and become a 'super-commuter'. He hoped that, despite his celebrity status, he would be accepted as a local by his new neighbours, although he joked that it would probably take twenty or thirty years. He was also keen to build on the farming he had learnt in Weston Turville and planned to get his hands dirty working on the estate. 'Farming has always been a love of mine and I shall be up at 6 a.m. in my wellies,' he said enthusiastically. 'I have already farmed for five years in Buckinghamshire, though we are obviously going to have to run the farm on a professional basis and get professional advice.'

Noel and Helen finally moved into Broomford Manor in early 1989. Noel wanted his parents near him, especially as his father was now in poor health. Dudley, who was 72, had prostate cancer and Noel wanted him where he could keep a concerned eye on him. So his parents sold their home in Tring and Noel installed them in a house in the next village, Exbourne, where Charlotte went to school. Noel, Helen and the girls lived in one of the farmhouses on the estate while improvements were made to the big house. Noel was determined that his children should have as normal an upbringing as possible and decided that six-year-old Charlotte would attend the local state school, followed by eighteen-month-old Lorna when she was old enough. This was something that Noel had insisted upon right from the beginning. Ray McGuirk explains: 'If ever Charlotte used Noel's name as a lever to get her own way at school or anywhere, he would really tell her off. As far as he was concerned, she had to be an ordinary person. She went to an ordinary school. All his children do.'

A new home wasn't the only change in Noel's life. Noel had gone to a lot of trouble and expense to fly all his friends up to his wedding in Scotland. But for many of them it was to be the last time they saw him: they would not be a part of his new life. Some accepted that he had simply moved on, while others were left wondering what they had done to fall from grace. One casualty of Noel's quest for a fresh start was his old friend Peter McMaster, whom he had known for fifteen years. Peter says, 'The last time I saw Noel was at the wedding. He went off on honeymoon for a few weeks; there was a certain amount of communication; and then that was it. I left messages that never got to him, or he didn't call back, and then I left a few more and still he didn't call. My wife and I sent him a Christmas card for about two years and didn't get any reply so in the end we stopped sending them.'

Peter agonised over his lost friendship and dissected every little detail in his mind, searching for a clue that might explain why Noel had cut him off. 'I went through a period of wondering if I had done something wrong,' he says. 'We were living in a one-bedroom flat in Windsor at the time and I felt it was very difficult to invite him back to our place because there was nowhere for him to stay. He could come to dinner but it would be very cramped because obviously we were living at a much lower level. I don't think Noel would have minded that and afterwards we felt that maybe we should have made the effort to invite him. But of course every time he invited us to the house it was usually with other people. Some weekends we'd go on our own but then we'd be doing things, like flying to the Grand Prix in his helicopter, and it's rather hard to get a helicopter off from a one-bedroom flat in Windsor. So, looking back, we thought that maybe it was that: maybe it was because we didn't actually reciprocate that well.'

But Peter soon discovered that he wasn't the only one of Noel's friends to have become *persona non grata*. 'Talking to our other friends, we realised that the same thing had happened to them, which was certainly a comfort. The bunch of friends that had known him from his first marriage to Gill, from way back, were broken off *en bloc*.' Peter suspects the reason why Noel drifted away from some of his old friends was because they had known Helen's predecessors, Debbie and Gill. He says, 'Once Helen came along there was very much a break with the "old" life. I don't think it had anything to do with the fact that we were all a lot older than her. I think it was because of the past. We must have been friends for more than ten years and I suppose it couldn't go on for ever. In the show-business world things move on, but I was sad about it because we'd had some good times. It was a very good period, but he just moved on. I'd very much like to get in touch with him again but I probably wouldn't be able to.'

And Paul Burnett, who had known Noel since he was nineteen, now hasn't seen him for more than ten years. He got the impression that Helen felt uneasy around Noel's friends: 'The last time I saw him was at Dave Lee Travis's house shortly after his marriage. I met his wife and she was very nice, very pleasant, but when you haven't seen people for a long time sometimes your lives have gone in different ways. I remember thinking that she didn't seem too comfortable with all Noel's old friends from his previous life. I quite understand why, because we used to be regular house guests, and I think when people get divorced the new wife tends to feel out of it if you socialise. I remember Noel saying to me, "This is ridiculous. We must keep in touch more often. It's silly to lose touch with old friends," and I think he meant that, too. Noel is something of a party animal, or was anyway. But even in these enlightened times we still rely on our wives to look after the social side of things, dinner parties and so on. Maybe it has more to do with her than him. I think Noel and Helen are quite insular and don't see many people. Part of the reason is that his fame is so extensive that he has to be like that. There are not many places he could go without being hassled because he's got such a recognisable face.'

While Peter McMaster and Paul Burnett were left wondering why they no longer saw Noel, the star's live-in handyman, Ray McGuirk, also noticed that Noel no longer saw many of the friends who had been such frequent visitors to the Manor House, and couldn't fail to notice that Helen, perhaps understandably, was determined that she and Noel should have a new start. 'We got on very well with Helen,' he reveals. 'But she did affect the whole of Noel's life – completely and utterly. She turned it upside down and she wanted nothing at all to do with his past.'

Ray recalls how Noel told him that their services were no longer required. 'We would have been quite happy to go with them down to Devon,' he says. 'But they wanted to change their lifestyle completely and they decided that they wouldn't have people living in as they had before. I suppose, to some extent, it was Helen. She was a younger person and she wanted to do what she wanted in life and make her mark on what was going on. She wanted nothing whatever to do with his past and that included me and my wife. Noel wasn't sad about letting us go. He had decided that that was what he was going to do in life, and at the end of the day we weren't family: we were employees.'

Ray, now a widower, was sad to be leaving after what he says were four wonderful years working for Noel. 'After we left I did miss it because we had a great deal of enjoyment working there. But I think Noel decided it was time to settle down and do something different in life. He wanted to be known as a businessman rather than an entertainer.'

Ray was shocked when he received a letter from the star giving him some bad news. 'There was nothing left of his past, even the animals,' says Ray sadly. 'A month after we left, Noel wrote and told me that they'd had to put down his Great Dane, Toast, because it had snapped at Charlotte.'

Ray remains devoted to Noel. 'He was not like a boss at all,' he says. 'He was a friend and we've remained friends. We don't talk to one another very often. He keeps changing his telephone number. He is such a very nice man, absolutely super. My wife died suddenly four years ago from a heart attack when she was 67. Noel didn't come to her funeral but he sent a donation. One of the things he used to miss was that he couldn't go to other people's weddings and funerals because if he went along to a wedding he was the centre of attention, not the bride and groom. It was the same with funerals and he appreciated this so he had to refuse them.'

Putting hundreds of miles between him and his old friends proved the final nail in the coffin of many of Noel's friendships. 'The move down to Devon really cut him off from everyone,' says Peter McMaster.

'I am afraid we don't see Noel now,' says Dave Lee Travis. 'He has locked himself away down in Devon and I haven't seen him for quite a long time. If Helen feels uncomfortable meeting friends from the old days, then that is something for Noel to deal with himself. You either keep in touch with people or you don't. There's no point in trying to figure out the reasons for it: that's just the way it goes. I don't miss him. I don't miss anybody socially if I don't see them. I just assumed he was a bit too busy to be gadding about with the people from the station. Maybe he's made new friends. I don't know why the hell he moved down there anyway. It's a bloody long way from where he was before.'

Noel, at this time, was keen to expand his business interests and in 1988 he recruited marketing consultant Andrew Dixon to promote the Unique Group. Dixon's Maidenhead-based firm, Marketing Activity, was hired to help Noel turn his numerous business ideas into reality. 'Noel wanted a guiding hand,' Andrew explains. 'He wanted to be able to bounce his ideas off somebody professional who understood the world of marketing. He needed to know which deals were worth it and which weren't, and he also wanted somebody to do the chores of an agent – blowing people out of meetings if he didn't want to go to them, cancelling deals and so on. He wasn't involved at that time with a manager or an agent, so the two were coupled together and we were appointed as marketing consultancy in support of Unique and Noel Edmonds.'

Their working relationship, says Andrew, was often a difficult one. 'When it comes to being professional at what he is paid to do, live television, Noel is outstanding and you can't criticise that,' he says. 'But, boy oh boy, when it comes to business and personality he's got a lot of flaws.' Andrew, a former officer in the Grenadier Guards, describes what being employed by the workaholic star was like: 'Noel would produce reams of ideas when he was away on holiday, flying his helicopter, or driving to the BBC. It was then down to us to turn them into reality. He had some good ideas, and he explained that all the ideas for his gameshows on television were his own. Noel admitted, "They are ludicrous ideas really, but if you present them properly they work." And I do think there's a certain amount of mileage in that. But he would never accept or understand that a project was not viable. He would not take no for an answer.'

Simon Cole, managing director of Noel's company Unique Broadcasting, bears much of this out. 'We've had our disagreements because I'm trying to slow Noel down,' he said. 'Given a free rein he'd be working 24 hours a day on 25 different ideas.'

Noel, claims Andrew Dixon, was also incredibly impatient. 'He didn't understand time at all. He would give me an idea for a book in September and expect it to be a pre-Christmas run: David Bellamy to have written it, me to have it sponsored, publishers to have done a deal, and for it to be distributed and out in the shops and away we go! A number of his ideas were very sensible but he just wouldn't wait the year for them to come to fruition. He would give me an idea to run with and then, because he got bored, he would fly off somewhere in his helicopter, spend two days in a hotel on the telephone arranging meetings with people – and then he'd call me and say, "I have managed in two days to get meetings with the following people. Why haven't you?" I felt he was always trying to show me up, and I found him impossible to work for.'

Noel's unpleasant experience at the hands of Basil Wainwright had understandably also made him cautious about investing any of his own cash in schemes, so much of Dixon's work involved finding backers.

But both men were strong personalities with their own way of doing things and it was an ill-fated relationship. Andrew explains: 'I found Noel a moody fellow, but I never gave him an inch and I was not ever going to be bullied or manipulated by him. He used to refer to me as "The Snobby Bastard" but he'd never say it to my face. He used to say it to the girls in the office and write it on notes. He certainly resented me, partly because he thought I spoke with a plum in my mouth and he didn't like people who'd been to public school. I think he was quite used to getting his own way with people and I didn't give him his own way at all, much to the annoyance of my own partners, who felt I should have been more humble with him because they wanted the business.'

Needless to say, the two men did not see each other more than they had to. 'It was a purely professional relationship and I didn't get involved that much with him socially,' says Andrew. 'You don't work with people and spend time with them without having a certain amount of social time together, but it always had a professional backdrop. On a couple of occasions he asked me to go down to Devon and I wasn't able to go, but it would have been work orientated if I had. The dates didn't suit me and I also didn't want to be in that position. If you are a house guest for two or three days you are going to have to spend some time together and I had worked out very quickly what he was like and where he was coming from. If you are a guest in somebody else's house you can't, if you have to, take the offensive with them. And I was always aware that the day might arise when I was going to have to tell Noel Edmonds where to get off, quite politely and professionally.'

After her marriage, Helen Edmonds was keen to familiarise herself with her husband's business interests, and during the period when Andrew was working for Noel she was often in attendance. 'When we had our meetings there would normally be a secretary, me, Noel and Helen,' he says. 'Helen was trying to become more involved. Nobody could be employed unless she hired them because she used to work in a recruitment consultancy. That's why she came to the meetings with us – she was effectively appointing us.'

According to another former business contact of Noel's, Helen didn't always dress in a manner suited to the office or boardroom. A naturally beautiful woman, she liked to look good, and, according to his friends, Noel encouraged her to dress in a sexy way. And some of her outfits would literally stop traffic and render Noel's business colleagues speechless. Said one former colleague, 'The very first time I met Helen was a warm summer's day and she turned up for a business meeting wearing a very light, see-through dress, with what appeared to be nothing underneath. They arrived at the heliport in London and she got out of the helicopter wearing next to nothing. It was obvious she didn't have a bra on. I actually think Noel likes her to look like that; he likes to have her on his arm. There were times when he would be all over her, and vice versa. It was almost a showing-off thing on Noel's part: "This is my jewel." '

Inevitably, Noel and Andrew Dixon parted company. 'It came to the logical conclusion that clearly we were not going to get along,' Andrew admits. 'We were sensible about it. I said to Noel, "You're not happy with what I'm doing; I'm not happy with the way you want me to do it; and I don't see how we can proceed." '

For the first couple of years following Michael Lush's death, Noel's television work had just been ticking over. His career had yet to fully recover from the tragedy and *Whatever Next?* ran for only one series. During the late 1980s, his BBC1 quiz, *Telly Addicts*, where members of the public showed off their knowledge of the nation's favourite programmes, was his only show, apart from his traditional festive offering, *Christmas Morning With Noel*. It wasn't until the autumn of 1988, two years after *The Late, Late*

*Breakfast Show* was pulled off the air, that he returned with a major new programme, *The Noel Edmonds Saturday Roadshow*, putting him on TV twice a week. By the following November, both the *Saturday Roadshow* and *Telly Addicts* were in the top-thirty most watched programmes and, while he was in the middle of negotiating his new BBC contract, it was rumoured that ITV had tried to tempt him away from the BBC by offering him £1 million to host *This Is Your Life* when Eamonn Andrews died. But Noel said modestly, 'I felt Eamonn was an impossible act to follow.'

His new three-year contract with the BBC cemented his position as one of the Corporation's top stars, and gave him the right to create and develop his own new shows. He was acknowledged to be one of broadcasting's most successful businessmen, and, as well as having his own TV production company and aviation businesses, he had made a comeback to the world of radio. He set up the Unique Broadcasting Company in October 1989 and established a lucrative deal with London-based Capital Radio to supply programmes to local radio stations.

Noel was also keen to expand his family, and shortly before Christmas 1989 he announced that Helen was pregnant again. Noel was overjoyed. He said the baby had been timed to coincide with a period when he wouldn't be busy working. 'It may sound calculating, but May–June is an ideal time to have a baby and it fits in with my work schedule,' he said.

Noel believed that moving to Devon was one of the best things he'd ever done, and said he didn't miss London or his show-biz friends at all. 'We have settled in well and we're very happy out here in the wilds,' he said.

Noel admitted that the locals had taken to calling him Lord Broomford, a title he was not displeased with. 'I can't sit in the House of Lords,' he joked. 'But because the previous owner of the house was a Lord Broomford the locals have decided I've inherited the title by maintaining the place as a farm.' However, the traditional country pursuits of hunting, fishing and shooting were not things that animal-lover Noel was interested in, and one of the first things he did when he moved in was ban the local hunt from coming across his land. 'I don't like animals being hurt,' he explained. 'The hunt took it quite well even though they'd been coming across here for centuries.'

Traditional family values were also high up on Noel's list of priorities. Despite having a TV presenter for a father, Charlotte and Lorna were discouraged from watching too much television. Launching a boardgame of *Telly Addicts*, a show wholly obsessed with the minutiae of TV trivia, he said, 'This sounds terribly twee, but we do entertain ourselves as a family. I have an aversion to turning on the TV to entertain the kids and keep them quiet. The temptation for parents to do that is enormous.' Charlotte was restricted to half an hour of television a night, consisting of programmes like *Blue Peter* and animal shows, and she and Lorna were encouraged to amuse themselves or play with their pets. 'She learnt from an early age that the TV is not something that goes on automatically,' said Noel. 'I am trying to encourage our children to be selective viewers.' Later, expanding on his theme, he indicated that he was one of the many people who feel television is to blame for a whole host of problems. 'A significant percentage of social ills are caused by that box in the corner,' he said seriously. 'There's a lot I don't want to expose my daughters to, and a lot of views are expressed that are not of any great value to society.'

As Ray McGuirk says, Noel was also keen that his daughters had as normal an upbringing as possible. 'I wouldn't want them cut off from the real world, as they are going to live in it eventually,' he said. 'It must be a problem for children of show-biz stars who live a celebrity existence, only ever mixing with their parents' famous friends. Our girls go to local schools and Helen and I don't mix in show-biz circles. We've lots of friends locally and they are very genuine. So I don't fear for our kids in terms of knowing what life's about.'

Noel may have been hoping for a boy, but their third child was another girl. Olivia was born in May 1990 and Noel quickly forgot all about wanting a son. 'Thank heavens for little girls,' he quipped as he and Helen proudly showed off their new daughter. At that time, Noel was lucky enough to spend long periods at home with Helen and the girls and work seldom took him away from Jacobstowe for more than a few days. 'But if I'm going to be away longer, I pack them all in the helicopter, baby as well, and off we go,' he said.

Shortly before Olivia's birth, and just eight months after saying that he'd never been happier, Noel took the unexpected step of putting Broomford Manor up for sale. In an amazing about turn, Noel said that he and Helen no longer wanted to live there. Friends said that Helen, who was only 28, often felt lonely and isolated miles from anywhere, especially when Noel was away in London. But Noel said that wasn't the case. 'It had nothing to do with that; Helen is simply not that sort of woman,' he said. 'The real reason we are leaving is that there are not enough hours in the day to do all the things we want to do here.'

It seemed that Noel and Helen had bitten off more than they could chew and discovered that their good-life dream of a rural idyll was not all it was cracked up to be. A few months before, in January 1990, while the family was away on holiday, fierce storms battered the Southwest of England and their estate suffered a huge amount of damage. 'We came back from a dream holiday in Florida to find that the hurricane had completely decimated the place,' the star explained ruefully. 'There were roofs off buildings, the main house was severely damaged and we had lost more than 2,000 trees. It was terrible. We were heartbroken.'

Running such a huge estate was an enormous responsibility and was also something of a tie. 'We sat down at the beginning of the year and thought through what we really wanted,' Noel explained. 'We knew we wanted to spend more time abroad – we hope to go to Australia in the near future – and we realised that it was impossible to do that with all our responsibilities here. We always felt we wanted to run this place ourselves. I'm not a lord-of-the-manor type who prefers to run his estate from a distance – we have always tried to be hands on. We have an estate manager and six staff but my wife does the main running of the place – she does all the books and she's learnt about sheep and fertilisers and VAT. And she has done it all with great aplomb. But when you've got three farms and all those responsibilities, it's hard to get away.' They were now looking for a more modest property, he said. 'Something smaller that we could leave quite easily.'

Helen said, 'Broomford Manor was everything we didn't want. We'd decided we were going to look for somewhere that was easy to manage and didn't need a thing doing to it. We had so much work done on our last house we never wanted to see builders again. So what did we buy? A place with fifteen bedrooms that hadn't been touched for sixty years!'

But, as they had discovered before, finding the right property was not easy. 'The problem with this part of the world is that it's short of interesting houses,' he complained. 'So we're not in a hurry and will only sell if we can find a buyer who is sympathetic to Broomford's unusual character.'

But six months later the Edmonds had yet another change of heart and pulled Broomford Manor off the market. They had failed to find anywhere that they liked as much as their home and had decided to stay put. Noel said, 'It's the old story of looking at loads of new places and discovering yours is best. All sorts of romantic things kept happening. We'd been off to see another house and when we came back the deer were standing on the drive, and I thought, Aah, you see, *they* don't want us to go. Then the locals kept coming up and saying, with hurt expressions, "Don't you like us? Don't you like it here?" We realised we love it here and there's nowhere better to bring up the children.'

But an outlying farm was sold off and, when Helen's mother Monica retired from her teaching job, she and her husband Dave left Reading and moved into a cottage on the estate to be near Helen and their grandchildren.

The last months of 1990 were difficult for Noel because he had to come to terms with the fact that his father was now desperately ill. Olivia's birth in May had brought the family some much needed respite from the worry and heartache of Dudley's battle against cancer, but the dark clouds descended again as his condition worsened. It was extremely hard for Noel because Dudley's illness coincided with an immensely busy period in his career. He was torn between a natural desire to be with his beloved father and a reluctance to let people down. An enormous amount of his time was spent helping to plan a giant helicopter event called HeliFest which was to be held the following year. Bob Limming, a friend whose company, Live Promotions, was organising the event with Noel, recalls how distressed Noel was by his father's ill health: 'He adored his dad and I remember he used to nip off to visit him and come back very depressed.'

Ray McGuirk, who was also a friend of Dudley's, reveals how the illness took hold: 'He was suffering when we were at Weston Turville. The cancer had spread up his back and he used to complain from time to time about how bad his back was. He went to the specialist but there was nothing anyone could do. In the end it spread up to his spine and that's what finished him off. It was a long, painful time.'

In November 1990, Dudley suffered a heart attack and was rushed to hospital in nearby Okehampton. He initially recovered and was allowed home, but suffered a relapse and was readmitted. Noel was worried sick, despite having to put on a brave face for that week's *Saturday Roadshow*. He said, 'All I want is to be with my dad. But that's impossible – I can't let everybody down. In the next three weeks I've got to fly to Scandinavia and then to America for my Christmas shows, but I'm worried in case anything happens while I'm away.'

Noel's worst fears were realised on 12 December 1990 when his father died. For 42 years Noel had looked up to and depended upon his dad, and now that he was gone Noel felt desolate. The person whose opinions and judgement he valued and trusted above everyone else's was now gone. The repercussions of this would be huge. Without Dudley's steadying hand to rein him in, Noel was cast adrift. As he battled to come to terms with his grief, Noel would be brought to one of the lowest points of his life.

# **10** House Party

NOEL WAS AT his father's bedside when he died and was able to say goodbye to him, something he was enormously thankful for. His nightmare scenario had been that his father would die when he was thousands of miles away. In the event, Dudley passed away barely 24 hours before Noel was due to catch a plane to America to film some scenes for his festive show, *Noel's Christmas Presents*. Poignantly, the programme featured children who were suffering from cancer and leukaemia. Noel was taking a group of them to New York for a Christmas treat. As he filmed scenes at BBC Television Centre with the youngsters, he had to take frequent breaks to telephone the hospital to see how his father was, and then return to the studio and put on a cheery face for his young guests.

After one such phone call, Noel was told his father's condition had worsened and doctors advised him to get to the hospital as soon as he could. In an agonising journey, Noel dashed from the BBC studios in London to Dudley's hospital bedside in Okehampton, Devon. He arrived in the nick of time. 'I got to the hospital about 45 minutes before he died,' he said later. 'Dad was conscious when I arrived. Helen and my mum were at his bedside, and I am so glad we were able to be there. Helen is convinced that he waited for me. I like to think that, too.'

Speaking of his grief a few weeks after his father's death, he revealed that the speed with which it happened had taken them all by surprise. He also said how difficult it had been to carry on with his Christmas show. 'Dad had had cancer for longer than he thought and his life expectancy was shorter than he had realised,' he said. 'We were halfway through making the programme when he died and it was especially difficult because a lot of children in the show suffered from cancer. For two days after Dad died I was devastated. I had never experienced death at first hand before and it hit me very, very hard. I closed off completely. I was so close to my dad. After he retired he came to work for me and we spent a lot of time together. Seven months earlier my daughter Olivia was born. I was at the birth and it was a fantastic thing to witness. Then, in December, there I was, watching my father die. It was like one door opening and another one closing.'

On top of his anguish, he also had a difficult decision to make: should he cancel the show and stay at home to grieve with his family, or should he go ahead with the trip to New York and give dozens of children a Christmas to remember? Noel was told by the BBC that no one would think any less of him if he chose to stay at home. 'My producer, Mike Leggo, was fantastic and said if I wasn't up to it they would scrap the show,' said Noel. 'That was an astonishing gesture as months of hard work and a lot of money had gone into it. There was no way I could let that all be thrown away and I decided the best tribute I could give my father would be to complete the show, regardless of how I felt. My dad taught me to be professional but to always work on my own terms. I have always tried to follow his advice, so I went to New York to film the final story. But my grief was still an astonishing burden. It was difficult to stop thinking about my father.'

Noel bravely managed to hide his pain as he filmed the jolly scenes for his Christmas special. Viewers watching at home on Christmas morning had no idea that the smiling and cheery star was in fact desperately unhappy. But as he sat down to watch the show with his family, the strain finally got to Noel and he burst into tears. 'I bawled my eyes out through the entire show,' he admitted. 'I couldn't believe Dad wasn't there. Every Christmas, Helen and I would go to church in the morning with Mum and Dad and our children, and we would get back in time to watch my programme. But this year there was an empty seat on the sofa. I just couldn't deal with it and I wept. The pressures of the previous few months suddenly hit me. I realised at that moment that my father's death was the lowest point in my life.'

Noel turned automatically to his wife. 'Helen was incredible throughout the whole period,' he said. 'She said to me then, "If you're ever going to have a nervous breakdown it will be now." But we got through it together and I think it probably strengthened our marriage.' Helen tried to make things as easy as possible for Noel by undertaking some of the more difficult tasks herself. It was she who went along and performed the grim duty of registering Dudley's death, and she also telephoned people to tell them the sad news.

Ray McGuirk recalls: 'Helen phoned me and we had a bit of a weep because he was such a super man; he really was.' And Noel's business associate Bob Limming tells how Dudley was liked by everyone who met him. 'He was a lovely man and we were all very sad when he died. His father was a very steadying influence on Noel – he used to rein him back when he got carried away, and his death hit Noel for six.' Noel was touched when dozens of villagers turned out for his father's funeral. 'There were thirty or forty people from our village,' he said proudly. 'Strangers who had never met my dad arrived to pay their respects. It was very moving.'

Noel said his father's dying had taught him that death was not something to be feared. 'The whole experience changed my attitude to death,' he explained. 'I'm not scared of it at all now. To use show-biz speak, I believe this life is just a rehearsal, or perhaps just a run-through.'

With his father gone, Noel felt even more protective towards his mother. 'When Dad was dying I had many conversations with him about it. I kept on telling him, "Don't worry. Mum will be all right." I firmly believe that with every experience in life you can turn a negative into a positive. Even the death of my own father – it brought Helen and my mother and I very close.'

Having decided to stay on at Broomford Manor, Noel and Helen threw themselves wholeheartedly into getting the property into shape. Referring to the time when they considered selling the estate as 'our mental aberration', Noel explained how things had got on top of them for a while: 'We'd lost a lot of trees in the storm; Helen was at a difficult stage in her pregnancy; and we were very down.' They were still living in the farmhouse, which they'd renovated, but the huge main house remained untouched. It hadn't had anything done to it for six decades and Noel reckoned it would take them at least five years to do it up. They were also faced with the daunting task of replanting thousands of trees, and a few months after the storm there had been another crisis, this time with their water – or, rather, the lack of it.

'Our water here is not very nice,' explained Noel. 'At different times it is different colours and because of the enormous influx of tourists quite often we have no water at all – we have droughts.' He decided they should try to get their own supply of fresh water and employed men to put a bore hole on the estate. The result was impressive and gave Noel an idea for a business venture. The star's aim was to grab a share of the lucrative bottled-water market and raise money to preserve plants and wildlife into the bargain. Thus Unique Sparkling Spring Water was born.

'The storm really made me think about where we lived, how lucky we are and how we should do as much as we can to protect the wonderful countryside that we have in Britain,' he said. 'The moment you actively get involved in forestry, preservation of wildlife and simple things like supplying your own water, it gives you a different perspective on life. I know it is a bit of a cliché, but a flower is for today and a tree is for ever. It's not what's in it for me; but what's in it for my girls – my little people. It represents a chance of a better world for them. I want my children to live in a world that is healthy and beautiful and not being destroyed by pollution. Anything I can do to help that has to be a good thing.'

But Noel Edmonds the single-minded businessman was also evident. He believed, he said, that one of the best ways he could help was by using his astute business sense to develop profitable projects to raise funds for the environment. 'I want to have a superb lifestyle so I have no intention of giving away money I have earned as Noel Edmonds,' he admitted frankly. 'I have an aversion to the tin-rattling philosophy. Projects that raise money for worthy causes have to be well balanced: all those involved must get something out of it.'

Apart from a tiny signature on the bottle label it would not be obvious to consumers that he had anything to do with Unique Sparkling Spring Water. 'I don't want people to say, "It's that bloody Noel Edmonds again, ramming things down our throats," ' he said. 'You have to be careful not to do that. I'm not trying to be goody two-shoes. It's not as if I give my BBC income to charity and in many ways I am still as selfish as the next person. But it's extremely exciting to be in business and have a third party benefit. People should be given the opportunity to vote with their wallets. With Unique there is no "green con", unlike some companies that enhance their bottom line by making profits out of so-called "environmentally friendly" products. It's a greedy world, but I believe companies have got to become more caring. The countryside has given me so much – changed my life in fact – that it's wonderful to put something back.' Profits from the water, which was sold in Sainsbury's, would go to the Woodland Trust.

Noel also launched *The Unique Guide to the Countryside*,

a book detailing country walks, the best spots for picnics and how to enjoy the countryside without damaging it. 'There wasn't a book that was fun and interesting, especially if you weren't an anoraked, booted hiker,' said Noel. 'It was originally going to be called *The Green Guide*, a coffee-table type book, but I realised that "green" was going to be synonymous with commercial abuse and cynical exploitation – which it now is.' The book would also raise money for the Woodland Trust, he said. He hoped to introduce a Unique Countryside Awards scheme for schools and companies, as well as organise a Countryside Week in June.

The marketing slogan for Unique Sparkling Water was 'There's a tree in every bottle'. But a friend tells how Noel's plan to give away a young tree to every purchaser went drastically wrong: 'The idea was to send everyone who bought a bottle of the water a sapling in the post. Noel bought 200,000 saplings and had them taken down to his estate. At the time he didn't have a lot of staff, and Helen was left with the task of watering them. He bought sleeves to send them out in and then went off and did all his other projects. But when he got around to sending them out the trees had grown. They would no longer fit in the sleeves so he couldn't post them. He ended up having to ditch 200,000 trees. Helen wasn't very pleased about that, having watered them and cared for them.'

The trees fiasco may well have been a portent of things to come. Four years after launching Unique Sparkling Water in a fanfare of publicity, the company went out of business with losses of almost £500,000. Noel had to bear the brunt of the collapse and the Woodland Trust – which Noel had forecast would receive £5 million – was left with just £15,000. It was a huge blow for Noel and an embarrassing setback in his quest to be respected as a serious businessman. *The Unique Guide to the Countryside* was an equally embarrassing flop, selling only an estimated 5,000 copies. Noel claimed that a major rival, whom he refused to name, had helped scupper his company by using its financial muscle to rob him of a £1 million distribution deal. And it was true that Unique Water's first year of trading had seen the full force of the recession. The international courier company DHL had stepped in halfway through with a huge cash injection to keep the company afloat, but in the end it was not enough.

The semiretirement which Noel had talked about at the end of 1989 had never really materialised. His television career was well and truly back on track and he spent the summer months excitedly working on a new, top-secret show that the BBC hoped would be the weapon with which they could topple ITV's *Blind Date* from the top of the Saturday-night ratings. That autumn, Noel would finally get the chance he wanted to take on Cilla Black's ratings-busting show and steal her crown. It would be his biggest challenge yet and, more importantly as far as he was concerned, it would be done live. In his opinion, that was the only way it should be done. 'Life's live; television should be live,' he said adamantly.

*Noel's House Party* hit the screen on 18 November 1991 and was an immediate success. Audiences and critics alike raved at the show's exciting format, particularly the feather in its cap – the revolutionary NTV. Millions of viewers watched spellbound as Noel pulled off the most astonishing trick on television: Claire Young, a 26-year-old nurse from Essex, was sitting in her mother's living room watching the show when suddenly she appeared on the screen, the first victim of NTV. Millions shared her surprise and the next week everyone was talking about NTV, wondering how it was done and whether they'd be next. Noel's new trick was deemed to be so brilliant that it had been kept secret from some of the show's own production staff. Even BBC bosses were kept in the dark to ensure that the stunt would be a surprise. 'We don't think it has ever been done before, not even in America,' Noel gushed. 'There have been loads of shows that use hidden cameras or have presenters surprising people by telephone or turning up on their doorstep, but

NTV is different because it is live. It goes way beyond *Candid Camera* because there is no prerecording or editing. I don't even have to leave the studio. This is why it has to be secret. The frightening thing for us is that we have got only one chance to get it right.'

Noel admitted that NTV was like something out of George Orwell's *1984*, in which people were spied on by hidden cameras. 'It's a bit like being Big Brother,' he said. 'I can speak to someone in their own home when they least expect it.' And he warned, 'If you don't come to the *House Party*, the *House Party* might just come to you.' It was people television at its very best – or worst. The cringe factor was huge: millions of TV viewers would see the unfortunate person slumped on the sofa, perhaps with a beer in their hand, or in curlers and a face pack, blissfully unaware that they were about to be beamed into the living rooms of Britain.

The TV star and DJ Chris Evans was the subject of a rumour that swept the media and show-business world that *House Party* had captured him on NTV while he was watching *Baywatch* on ITV. Apparently, the clip could not be shown on family television. The most often asked question about the show remains: 'Is it true about Chris Evans and *Baywatch*?'

By and large, the response was good, very good; although some of the other games on the show were sneered at. The *Independent*'s TV critic, Giles Smith, wrote, 'What really took you back was when two contestants, with their hands tied, bobbed for objects in a bucket of liquid. This game was already tiresome when Brueghel was alive, and might reasonably be thought a form of entertainment that television was invented to spare us. Tune in next week when Noel discovers what fun you can have with an inflated pig's bladder.'

Radio 1 DJ Steve Wright said scathingly, 'In an age when people like Tony Slattery and Mike McShane, Clive Anderson and Clive James can make it as television presenters, less sharp-end personalities like Noel Edmonds seem old hat. Noel is a professional presenter, but he's still doing now what he did in 1982.'

But, most importantly, viewers loved *House Party*. During one programme the month after its launch, 1.25 million people attempted to ring in, jamming the BBC switchboard and setting a new television phone-in record. It was a triumph for people TV. The show had already managed to beat ITV's *Blind Date*, and the ratings were up as high as 13.2 million. Occasionally things went wrong, but often the mistakes would trigger yet more response from the audience. Noel said, 'I tripped up one week and fell on my face and people sent me sticking plasters through the post with comments like "Try taking more tonic with it". We had a bit of a disaster another week with a miserable policeman, but the viewers seem to enjoy it when things go wrong.'

Noel, at the age of 43, was riding high and was more popular than ever. *Radio Times* readers voted him Sexiest Male TV Presenter (he narrowly beat newsreader Martyn Lewis). Noel proclaimed *House Party* to be the most successful show he had ever worked on. 'I really think *Noel's House Party* is something new,' he boasted. 'It's a happy coincidence, after the huge wave of criticism for the BBC, that here we are getting these figures. But it's right for the time and, if, in years to come, people said that was the start of a new age in BBC light entertainment, wouldn't it be wonderful?'

The powers that be at the BBC breathed a huge sigh of relief when *House Party* shot up the ratings chart. The results were a port in the storm for the Beeb, which for months had languished a dismal ten points behind ITV in the ratings. Now it was ITV's turn to take a pasting as Noel kept Cilla's *Blind Date* right down the charts.

*House Party* also built on the success of *The Late, Late Breakfast Show*'s Hit Squad and his *Roadshow*'s Gotcha Oscars. But this time it wasn't unsuspecting members of the public who found themselves being hit upon by Noel and his team, but equally unsuspecting celebrities. This gave Noel a chance to wind up some of his former colleagues by making them unwitting victims of a Gotcha. Two of his first targets were his former Radio 1 colleagues Dave Lee Travis and David Jensen.

When *House Party* showed the now legendary Gotcha on DLT, it pulled in the show's biggest ever audience. More than 15 million tuned in to watch Dave get stitched up by Noel. And, as DLT was forced to admit, Noel got him in a *big* way. In fact, he describes it as the worst moment in his 26-year radio career. He recalls: 'I must have said to him at some point that he'd never get me and that would have been like a red rag to a bull.' Noel set Dave up during a live radio broadcast by replacing the usual pub team in DLT's weekly phone-in quiz contest with himself and two actors. They pretended to be so stupid they couldn't answer a single question and, as the minutes dragged on and the answers got more ridiculous, Dave grew more and more frustrated. After twenty minutes it had turned into a nightmare for DLT, who thought his show was heading for disaster.

'I often asked contestants to turn their radios down while they were talking to me because otherwise you get this dreadful feedback,' says DLT. I later found out that Noel had a radio in his hand next to the phone, and it was making a horrible noise. The quiz was meant to last 8 minutes but it took 25. I was tearing my hair out by the end. The answers to my questions were terrible. I remember asking, "Where would you find a dead man's handle?" and getting the answer, "A hearse?" I pissed myself laughing at the start but after that I just put on a record and said on air, "I'm just going away to rethink my entire career."' At that moment, Noel raced round from a nearby office and burst into Dave's studio – where he was confronted by an enraged, red-faced DLT ready to explode.

Dave recalls: 'I went mad. Noel had to edit out most of my reaction when he screened the Gotcha on his show because I was furious. My language was terrible.' It was,

DLT says, the only time he had ever wanted to hit anyone. 'I saw Edmonds' beaming face and I wanted to hit him – very hard.'

It was all the more embarrassing for DLT because it wasn't the first time that he had fallen for one of Noel's pranks. He admits sheepishly, 'After I took over the Radio 1 *Breakfast Show* from Noel, I was preparing the programme one day when the phone went. I picked it up to hear this well-spoken female voice saying she was from the BBC administration department. She said she was asking all the staff if they had a television licence because the BBC had to be seen to be setting an example. I said I did, and then she asked if she could see it. I said, "For God's sake, I don't carry it around with me like a credit card." But she ignored me and asked for my licence number, so I lost my temper and shouted, "What's your name?" Back came the reply: "Dave, it's Noel Edmonds." I came out with a load of filthy language because I knew he would put it on his show. All you could hear at the end was bleep, bleep, bleep, like a Morse code message from hell. I was quite steaming simply because I'd fallen for it, which is a bit sad really.'

Noel wasn't so lucky when he tried to spring a Gotcha on David Jensen. The former Capital Radio DJ, who now works for Heart FM, immediately spotted he was being set up, although he didn't realise that it was his old flatmate from Radio Luxembourg who was behind it. He explains: 'I was asked to go along and do some TV commercials but when I got to the studio I thought, There's something not quite right about this. The products were so obviously bogus: one was an ice cream on a stick and the stick was hollow, or something ridiculous like that. Then there was a greatest-hits holiday album with somebody called Theodora Popolopodos, who was supposed to be the biggest-selling European singer. I immediately suspected something was weird. I'd never heard of such a person, and even if I didn't like them I would at least be aware of the name. There was another one where they wanted me to advertise a new razor for five o'clock shadow. But I'm the fairest person on this planet: I could have five o'clock shadow for a week and no one would notice, so I said no.

'They tried, and cajoled and threatened and got angry. But I knew I was being set up. Unfortunately I thought it was Jeremy Beadle and not Noel Edmonds. I suppose I should have been a better sport, but I didn't realise it was Noel at the time. I said, "I'm sorry, but you're going to have to find someone else," and I just walked away. Then Noel came out and I thought maybe he'd been asked to go and do some of the stupid stuff as well. I didn't realise he was behind it, and said, "Hey, Noel, what are you doing here?" It turned out that the guy who apparently owned the company that made these products had been Noel in disguise. But it just didn't work.'

Noel, says David, lost his sense of humour when his stunt backfired. 'He was OK – he wasn't unfriendly – but maybe he was a little bit miffed,' he says. 'I don't think he was pleased that it hadn't gone well. I suppose they'd invested a lot of time and effort in setting the thing up, only for it not to work. But if I had known it was for Noel I probably would have pretended and gone along with it. I suspect more people spot it and go along with it than we know, but I didn't know it was for him. I hadn't seen him for about four years. It was completely out of the blue, which is why I didn't suspect him. I immediately thought it was Jeremy Beadle because I had seen him at functions to do with Capital over the years.'

There was another fiasco when *House Party* tried to set up *Newsnight* presenter Peter Snow. Noel and the team sat outside his home for hours before realising he had moved house. And Noel said that the language that came out of the normally mild-spoken Nicholas Parsons when he was Gotcha'd was so filthy that he has the dubious title of being the show's champion bleeper.

Former colleagues of Noel felt they had to be constantly on their guard in case they were next on his list. DJ John

Peel admits to existing in a perpetual state of paranoia, constantly expecting Noel to jump out on him. 'For some reason he's determined to get me,' complained Peel. 'Any invitation I get, I think, Is Noel behind this?' The only attempt to get me that I know about was when he genuinely thought that I was stupid enough to want to take part in a nature programme in which the idea was that I would stay up all night on a badger watch. The joke was that they weren't going to be real badgers: they were going to be people with glove puppets. I thought, Is that the best you can do?'

Noel's Gotchas are rumoured to have cleaned up the industry. Faced with a duff film crew or an event that keeps going wrong, actors don't dare to throw a luvvie tantrum in case Noel pops out at them. Jonathan King even turned down £70,000 to do a watch commercial because he mistakenly believed it was a joke by Noel. If King and Peel are paranoid they aren't the only ones. Noel too has confessed to the odd sleepless night spent worrying about what his 'victims' would do to get their own back on him. As prankster *par excellence*, he realised he was an obvious target for a dose of his own medicine. 'Let's face it, there are an awful lot of people who would like nothing better than to see me get my comeuppance,' he said. 'Every time I go on a business engagement, I'm worried that it will be a setup to get back at me. I've lifted pictures on walls and looked behind mirrors – I'm turning into a paranoid lump! I have become so cautious that I have even done an inch-by-inch search of my hotel room, fearing the worst. When I was in Manchester on business I returned to my hotel at about 10 p.m. and found I had been moved to another room. Reception said that they had upgraded me but I was immediately suspicious. The new room just didn't seem right. I looked at the bathroom and the lounge area and some of the dimensions seemed wrong. I thought, Someone could get a camera crew into that space. What the hell's going on? I paced the rooms from wall to wall, measuring them, and was convinced it was a setup. I slept with my underpants on that night.'

It wasn't only Noel's Gotchas that entertained viewers. His choice of clothes over the years has also been the source of much hilarity and provided television critics with a never ending means of ridiculing him. Luridly coloured tops have become synonymous with Noel Edmonds. The most often asked question in interviews and fan mail is: 'Where do you buy your jumpers?' The star takes it in good part and cheerfully admits to having no fashion sense at all. The clothes he wears on *House Party* are chosen with the help of a stylist from the BBC's wardrobe department who takes him on whistle-stop tours of designer shops to put together outfits. 'I stand there feeling like a schoolboy being kitted out at the beginning of term,' he said. And he admitted his height – he is just 5 feet 5 inches tall – also causes problems. 'It's no good trying to put me in Armani suits, for instance, because I'm too short to carry them off. It looks as though somebody else should be in there with me!'

Off screen, Noel wears suits by Yves St Laurent for business. When he's not working, he prefers the country-squire look of tweed jackets and cavalry twills. He buys these from the Cornish gentleman's outfitters Coombes of Bude, a shop with strong family connections, run for many years by Helen's grandfather Bert Soby. Helen used to help out behind the counter when she was young.

Noel has also come into criticism for keeping the same image for three decades. His now greying hair is still highlighted blond and cut in the same style, and the beard is omnipresent. He was once referred to as 'that rare breed, the multimillionaire with the exhaust-fitter's haircut'. Paul Burnett offers an insight into why Noel has steadfastly refused to update his image. 'TV people have to keep the same look,' he explains. 'Noel has got such a recognisable face that if he shaved off his beard it would make headlines. That's the image – that's the product. It's like Jimmy Savile and Tony Blackburn: they keep that look because that's the product. Also, comedians start picking up on you and you become a kind of figure of fun. But I'm sure Noel doesn't mind – he's laughing all the way to the bank.'

Noel has admitted his wife would like him to shave his beard, but acknowledges that it might not go down well with viewers. 'It's a trademark and it might distract the viewers if I shaved it off,' he said. 'They would be too concerned with looking at my chin and not paying attention to the show. To a point, I'm a manufactured product. It's hard to market myself when there is me the presenter, me the private person and how others see me. Try to identify yourself out of that mess! I don't claim I've got it right.'

*House Party*'s main appeal was that it was first and foremost a family show and appealed right across the spectrum. People of all ages and classes watched it. Noel found it easy to come up with ideas for the show because he was, at heart, a family man. But Noel also confided that he and Helen were careful to make time for themselves as a couple, away from the girls – what he chose to call 'dirty weekends'. 'I have a very attractive wife and I want to be able to enjoy all aspects of her,' he said in an interview with the *Sun*. 'I don't play much sport but I hump for Britain.' And when he and Helen met a journalist from the *Sunday Mirror* for an interview at an exclusive country-house hotel, Noel allegedly pointed to one of the upstairs rooms and said, 'See that window? We gave that room a right seeing-to.'

*House Party* continued to go from strength to strength, doing well against everything that ITV put up against it. ITV rescheduled its line-up four times to try to woo back viewers: *Barrymore, Family Fortunes, Beadle's About* and *Baywatch. House Party* audiences rose to 15 million. In autumn 1992, ITV tried putting the might of its successful and popular new show, *Gladiators*, head to head with Noel.

'I think it's going to be tough,' Noel conceded. 'I don't think that *Gladiators* will be an easy rival to deal with.' *Gladiators* had just pulled in a massive 13 million viewers, but, up against *House Party*, 2 million viewers defected to Noel. When the audience viewing figures were published, *House Party* was celebrating a lead of almost 1 million.

Up to 30,000 people wrote in to the show every week requesting a setup for their family or friends. Researchers would then spend three weeks making certain that whoever they picked would have the right temperament and wouldn't end up punching Noel. Asked to explain why he thought so many people wanted to be on the show, the star said, 'We live in an anonymous world where people are desperate for their fifteen minutes of fame.'

On the *House Party* broadcast on 24 October 1992, Noel disguised himself as a bright-pink monster to surprise dancer Wayne Sleep. The audience chuckled away, not yet realising the implications of what they were seeing. Mr Blobby was spawned.

# 11 Blobbymania

N MARCH 1993, *Noel's House Party* was voted Best Light Entertainment Programme by the British Academy of Film and Television Arts. Receiving the BAFTA at a glittering ceremony at London's Grosvenor House Hotel was, said Noel, the proudest night of his life. A foal, bred by Helen and born the day of the award, was promptly named Bafta.

But the glory of being recognised as something special by the TV industry failed to stop the criticisms that were being levelled at the show. It made people look silly, critics said; it relied too heavily on embarrassing people to get laughs; Noel was annoying. *House Party* was watched by up to 13 million people – or, as the satirical magazine *Private Eye* sneeringly put it, 'by every moron in the country'. The social commentator AN Wilson described it as 'the modern equivalent of hell', the personalities trapped in the studio 'like the tormented souls in Dante'. Victor Lewis-Smith, a comedian and TV critic, said of Noel, 'I think he's a cynical piece of shit. He makes my blood boil. God knows what he does, but I wish he wouldn't. I wish he'd do us all a favour and have an ejector seat fitted in that helicopter of his. A hundredweight of salami and no Noel Edmonds seems a fair swap to me.' Fellow critic Tony Parsons said that Noel should be beaten to death with a baseball bat.

The scathing remarks annoyed Noel. 'I don't humiliate people,' he said defiantly. 'I've got a gland that says, "Enough. Stop short of humiliation." Embarrassment is funny; distress is not. I know how far to go. You wouldn't believe the number of people who actually ask to come on the show and be covered with gunge. People like Robert Kilroy-Silk, Mary Whitehouse and Edwina Currie have all volunteered. They know it says you have a sense of humour and you are all right.' Noel was trying not to take the criticisms personally. 'You have to be philosophical in this game,' he reasoned. 'When you have a hit show the only thing they can knock is me. Of course it's not pleasant but, in general, people are so nice to me. A taxi driver who had seen the Christmas show refused to take a fare from me. He said he'd been so moved by the things we did – giving things away and reuniting people. And who does get praise in popular television? There is an elitist, snobbish view, which is actually also stupid because it ignores the requirements of a very large percentage of the population.'

Whatever people said, and however much they scoffed, Noel was the one who had the last laugh because his show was a runaway success. People of all ages and from all social classes tuned in. '*House Party* has been hugely satisfying because the A, B and C breakdowns are equal,' he said. 'The age range is three to ninety-three and the sex is balanced. Men think I'm unthreatening and it appeals to them because they think of setting up their mates.' Given the knocks he'd had, no one could blame Noel if he sounded faintly smug. And, as well as huge viewing figures for *House Party*, he had another feather in his cap as far as the BBC was concerned. The show's Audience Index – the AI factor as it is known in television – was extremely high. Audience Index is deemed to be even more important than actual viewing figures because it represents how many people like what they are watching. *Noel's House Party*'s AI Index was 80 per cent – higher than most of the other big weekend shows, including *Gladiators* and *Beadle's About*. 'That puts us in the same league as *The Two Ronnies* and *Blackadder*,' said Noel proudly. 'That is why the programme is so important to the BBC, and why the Controller of BBC1, Alan Yentob, cites it as an example of how you can bring together quality and quantity.'

It came as no surprise, therefore, when in May Noel signed an exclusive contract with the BBC which would earn him an estimated £10 million over the next four years. Once again, rumours abounded that he had been thinking of defecting to ITV. Reports claimed he had give the Beeb a 24-hour ultimatum: either deliver a deal to his liking, or lose him. 'This man is a unique talent,' said Alan Yentob, announcing the new four-year deal. 'Noel is committed to the BBC – people don't do things just for the money.' Yentob went on to describe *House Party* as 'the most important show on BBC'. The deal made Noel the BBC's most expensive signing and the second-highest-paid television star, after Cilla Black. It was a complex deal which represented far more than just an annual salary for the star, and his companies Unique Broadcasting and Unique Television were heavily involved. Unique owned the rights to *House Party* and *Telly Addicts* and Noel would make more money from programme merchandising, books and toys, and by selling rights to foreign channels to make their version of *House Party*.

He was also getting more involved in building up his business empire and increasingly had his fingers in many pies. Not all of his schemes would be successful. During the 1990s several of his business involvements would hit problems. Infuriatingly for Noel, these failures would attract more attention than his many successes. Being a household name proved to be something of a double-edged sword, for it meant that would-be partners, dazzled by the kudos of going into business with such a well-known celebrity, would end up resentful and disappointed if Noel failed to perform miracles.

During 1993, Noel was also cashing in on another lucrative spin-off from his TV show with a series of outdoor events which he called *Noel's Garden Party*. This was basically *House Party* on the road and during the summer months Crinkley Bottom was re-created at Doncaster and Haydock Park racecourses. Helicopters inevitably played a part, with precision flying displays, and other attractions included a village fair complete with jugglers, strongmen, stilt walkers and magicians, and a host of games from the TV show. Visitors would have the chance to be dunked in the gunge tank, or share the secrets of their home life by letting their children be interviewed in Wait Till I Get You Home. And, of course, there was also the possibility of meeting Mr Blobby.

Nobody, probably Noel included, had realised just how big Mr Blobby would become. Less than a year after his first appearance, the people of Britain were in the grip of Blobbymania. The giant seven-foot-tall pink and yellow rubber creation with rolling eyes and a silly grin became a national obsession, popular with kids and adults alike. The ludicrous, skittle-shaped character, who specialised in flinging himself on people – a practice known as being 'Blobbied' – was to become an enormous money-spinner for Noel. Quick to spot an opportunity, Noel saw endless possibilities: Mr Blobby balloons, Mr Blobby T-shirts, Mr Blobby everything really. Despite the fact that Blobby was invented not by Noel but by *House Party* producer Michael Leggo, it was Noel who owned the copyright, on a 50–50 basis with the BBC. Although it had been Noel who first donned the monstrous rubber suit, it was immediately apparent that viewers wanted to see Noel and Blobby on stage together. Shakespearean actor Barry Killerby was hired to 'be' Blobby.

Noel held four *Garden Parties* that year, which he hoped would attract a total of 100,000 people, and had a further ten planned for 1994. BBC televised the Haydock Park event over the August Bank Holiday weekend. As Noel arrived by helicopter, he was immediately upstaged by a very special guest. The crowd went mad, chanting his name over and over, 'Mr Blobby, Mr Blobby, Mr Blobby . . .', as Blobby climbed out of his very own Blobbycopter – painted pink and yellow like him. Upward of 22,000 people jostled and nudged each other in a bid to catch a glimpse of Noel and his peculiar pink sidekick. One person observed that, from a short distance away, Blobby smelt like a giant condom. Not all the punters were happy bunnies, especially when their attempts to get near their idols ended in frustration. Some complained that Noel was often nowhere to be seen, or was surrounded by security guards, and that Mr Blobby was similarly elusive at times. But, on the whole, people had a good time and Noel joked that Blobby had needed four minders to stop him being mobbed – two more than him.

Crinkley Bottom, the fictitious setting for *House Party*, was in fact based on Noel's own home. He confessed that his house had provided the inspiration for the show. 'There is part of me that lives at Crinkley Bottom all the time,' he said. 'There is a definite link. The *House Party* set reminds me very much of Broomford Manor, although the set designer has never been down here. Letters are delivered regularly addressed to Noel Edmonds, Crinkley Bottom, Devon. And, the other day, a signpost mysteriously appeared in the village with an arrow pointing THIS WAY TO CRINKLEY BOTTOM.' It wasn't just his house he'd borrowed ideas from either – the West Country locals had provided him with a wealth of possibilities too. He admitted that ideas for the show were sparked by characters and situations they'd encountered in Devon. 'We've got to be fairly careful in that respect,' said Noel diplomatically. 'A local farmer was convinced that one of the Crinkley Bottom characters was based on him. He collared me in the village and said, "You girt bogger! That were me on telly, warn't it?" As he was talking about the village-idiot character I was anxious he might be offended. But he seemed chuffed: he was famous at last!'

During the early 1990s, when the recession was at its worst, Noel's helicopter company, Unique Aviation, had started to feel the pinch as fewer and fewer companies were able to afford its services. Noel had also got rid off his own helicopter, concerned that he had too many financial commitments to afford to run it. But, with the success of *House Party*, it was a luxury he felt able to indulge in once again. In 1993, he bought himself a six-seater 700hp jet engine Squirrel, costing £500,000. He could well afford it. Blobby alone was making him a fortune in spin-offs. In 1994, Blobby grossed £30 million and, on average, the star received £1.9 million a year in profit from the pink blob. At Christmas 1993, Mr Blobby stormed up the charts with his debut record. And in March 1994, Noel won another prestigious award when he was voted Top BBC Personality at the Radio and Television Industry Club's awards in London.

In October 1994, costume designer Dominic Murray claimed that he had designed Mr Blobby and the copyright belonged to him, not the BBC. The Beeb robustly denied this and said that Blobby had been made in the BBC's own props department. Mr Murray complained that he could not afford to pursue his claim through the courts because he didn't have enough money. It was the second month running that Mr Blobby was at the centre of unwelcome publicity. The *Sun* revealed that a blonde model who starred in a video alongside the kiddies' favourite had appeared naked in a soft-porn magazine. 'Mr Blobby's Girlie in Lesbian Romp,' screeched the headline. But Blobby was attracting some good publicity too. Noel set up the Dr Blobby Tour Charity so the pink favourite could visit sick children in their hospital beds. 'It's about Mr Blobby bringing a little cheer into some people's lives,' said Noel. 'The visits were being done informally before, but we've seen the difference Blobby makes so now we will be doing organised trips.'

Travelling the country and talking to 400 children a year for the Wait Till I Get You Home segment in *House Party* provoked a more serious side to the star. In an interview with *Radio Times* he said he believed that 'a significant percentage of social ills' were caused by television, and that meeting so many kids had given him an amazing insight into the state of British family life. A rarely glimpsed, serious Noel, who had been brought up to believe in family values, had clearly been upset by what he'd seen and heard. 'It is deeply disturbing,' he admitted. 'I don't know what we can do because the fundamentals of society are wrong. There is no guidance from the top and moral values have been eroded. It's incredibly easy to make a baby and incredibly difficult to bring up a child to be a responsible adult. There is nothing wrong with single mothers, but they undoubtedly benefit from having a stable relationship with a man. There is also the decline in educational standards. Eight out of ten children under the age of ten can't read properly.'

It was serious stuff and more what you would expect from a politician than from the presenter of a prime-time light-entertainment programme. Such remarks may well have been what prompted the *Daily Express* newspaper to pose the question: 'Is the time right for Noel's House (of Commons) Party?' With tongue firmly in cheek, the paper suggested that the star had all the necessary clout to make an excellent, high-profile Member of Parliament, and even claimed he had a clause in his contract entitling him to quit his contract with the BBC should he decide to stand for election. It wasn't Noel who had put the clause in, the paper explained, but the BBC, who did not, apparently, think that anyone could be an entertainer and an MP. Noel, however, showed no indication of being attracted to a life in politics as he was much too busy being Mr Saturday Night.

Prime-time weekend television is a tough world and it was perhaps inevitable that *House Party* could not go on achieving such fantastic viewing figures for ever. After bathing in the warm glow of success for almost four years, Noel felt a nasty draft as *Blind Date* whizzed past his ears to become Saturday teatime's top-rating show. By the end of 1995, the honeymoon appeared to be over for *House Party*. Even those critics who had previously loved the show now reluctantly conceded that it had become 'boring' and peopled with has-been 'C-list' celebrities. The *Evening*

*Standard*'s TV reviewer Matthew Norman wrote about Noel, 'Once considered innovative and creative, he has become smug, arrogant and complacent . . . whose peculiar skill is to construct formulae, prove their effectiveness, and then repeat them ad nauseum.' The audience appeared to agree: *House Party* had lost 3 million viewers since its heyday in 1992, and had now fallen 2 million behind *Blind Date* in the ratings.

It was the start of a difficult period for Noel. Some of his business dealings were also making unwanted headlines. Unique Sparkling Water had gone embarrassingly bust, and the star's latest venture, into theme parks, was fraught with difficulties. In December 1995, he announced he was suing Lancaster City Council over the closure of his World of Crinkley Bottom theme park at Morecambe. The park had opened in July 1994 as a joint venture with the council to bring tourists to the ailing seaside town. The council closed it just four months later, but the ensuing legal battle, which lasted for two years, would see Noel emerge as the victor.

Another theme park, at Cricket St Thomas, in Chard, Somerset, was also experiencing problems. Crinkley Bottom was re-created alongside a beautiful wildlife and leisure park on a 1,000-acre park owned by the Taylor family. John Taylor had bought the estate in the 1960s and the main house was the elegant eighteenth-century mansion that was featured in the BBC comedy *To the Manor Born*. Cricket St Thomas was an attractive and tranquil setting and perhaps one not entirely suited to the brash style of Blobbyland. Stephen Taylor, John's younger brother, explains why the family decided to go into business with Noel: 'Noel made an appeal on television and in the press in November 1993 to start a leisure business in the West Country. He didn't want to start up a theme park from scratch; he wanted to run it in conjunction with somebody else. We knew he had a house just outside Exeter and realised that he was liable to do this on our patch, so we took the decision to see if we could join him rather than beat him. Noel thought our place was fantastic. We'd just built some little houses which he thought linked in with the Crinkley Bottom theme, and, in turn, we thought being associated with him could make us a national attraction, rather than just a regional one.'

Crinkley Bottom at Cricket St Thomas was hailed as 'Britain's first TV leisure park'. 'The first year we got a huge amount of publicity and an extra 100,000 people came,' says Stephen.

But after the success of the first year, disenchantment set in and in 1996 the arrangements came to an end, although the Taylors did not finally settle all their debts until 18 months after that time. The Taylors say their deal with Unique was never properly completed because of disagreements over how the partnership was to be funded and how the profits should be carved up. Unique, in turn, say they lost confidence in the Taylors. Unique argue that the relationship had got off to a disastrous start because despite written assurances that all planning consents had been obtained and would be obtained for all proposed developments, and that all relevant health and safety legislation was complied with, within the first six months the *Sunday Express* had done a double-page exposé on the poor health and safety standards at the Park and another major exposé quickly followed, revealing how no planning permission had been sought for all the new buildings. Cricket St Thomas kept Mr Blobby and the Taylors paid to do so, but in the latter half of 1997, the family put Cricket St Thomas up for sale.

Noel had also gone into business at Bicton Park, East Budleigh, Devon, which was run by Steve Stevens. When Bicton closed in 1997, Noel issued a press release which said, 'I am personally delighted that the Stevens have gone out of business.' The day that Steve and his wife Jenny left Bicton Park was, according to Noel, 'a Red Letter day for tourism in the West of England'. The star's words were like salt in the wound for Stevens, with whom the star is embroiled in a bitter legal dispute.

Steve Stevens admits Bicton was already struggling when he and his wife took it over, but claims that, by sheer hard work, they had managed to increase the number of visitors. In 1996, when they were offered the opportunity to go into business with Noel Edmonds, they couldn't believe their luck. 'I had a phone call from a girl who was looking at sites for Edmonds and she made an appointment for him to come,' explains Steve. 'He spent four hours looking around the park and we later received a lovely glossy book and a personally signed letter from him. We believed that once his ame was above the gate there were going to be thousands of people coming in.'

Like others before him, Stevens hoped that Noel held the key to boosting his business, and readily agreed to go into partnership with the star and transform Bicton Park into Gotchaland. 'We opened on 11 July 1996 and closed down before the end of September,' he says glumly. 'From day one everything went wrong. It was a total bloody mess.' The main theme of the park was the Gotcha: 'Nothing is what it seems' or 'What you see is not what you get'. But, says Steve, the visitors didn't appreciate the joke. 'The brochure mentioned zoos, speedboat rides and dinosaurs, but when they arrived there was nothing,' he explained. 'It was a Gotcha but it's not funny, especially when you've paid £4.85 to get in. Kids couldn't see the funny side: they started crying when there were no animals and a pile of sticks in the cage where the stick insects were supposed to be.'

Other signs heralded nonexistent attractions, such as speedboat rides which departed at 9.30 a.m. and 6.30 p.m. – when the park was open from 10 a.m. to 6 p.m. 'I asked Edmonds about it and he said, "Well, it's a Gotcha. People should know it's a Gotcha. You've got to be expecting to be tricked," ' Steve says. 'But it was a one-off joke. My thirteen-year-old son walked around the park and said, "Well, it's all right, Dad, but you wouldn't come back and see it again." ' Older visitors, many who came to see Bicton's fine formal gardens, were not impressed, he claims.

Unique, however, stress that it was never an element of the theme of Bicton Park that the public would be tricked to come to the park believing they were going to see one thing, and see another. Had Unique been shown the brochure before it was sent out, as they should have been, Unique would have ensured that it only promoted items that had already been built. Unique also stress that the only reason items were not in the park was because the Stevens had not invested sufficient funds to ensure that certain other elements that were promoted in the leaflet were built in time. Unique did not want to continue the relationship with the Stevens and so terminated the agreement, and on the advice of their lawyers, issued bankruptcy.

Bicton Park is now closed, and Stevens, who runs a pub in Budleigh Salterton, Devon, admits the strain of the past two years spent battling with Noel has taken its toll on his family. 'I can't concentrate on anything. I'm a nervous wreck,' he says. 'It's upsetting my wife and it's getting to the kids too. We could lose our home because we live on the park.'

Terry Williams, who runs a go-kart and ride manufacturing business in the West Country, is experienced in the leisure industry and attempts to shed some light on the fallings-out that have punctuated some of Noel's ventures into theme parks. 'Noel Edmonds is entering into the leisure industry with an entertainment background and the two things are not the same,' he explains. 'It's a real can of worms but it all boils down to the fact that if you go into something – like the Stevenses did with Noel Edmonds – and it has failed, human nature is not to blame yourself: it's to blame someone else. Looking at it from Edmonds' point of view, a lot of people have said, "Oh great, I'm in with Noel Edmonds," without stopping to ask themselves exactly what he is providing. And what he's providing has not been very much; he is just providing his name. Some have jumped on the bandwagon and become starstruck, perhaps thinking he is going to be a rescue mission for them, whereas, in reality, like everything else in this world, it takes a lot of hard work.

'Three of the five parks have closed amid rows. The only place it has ever really worked is at Pleasurewood Hills in Great Yarmouth, where they have Peter Haddam, who is one of the best site directors that anybody could wish for. They have used Edmonds' equipment as a basic idea and improved upon it, whereas others expected it to be their saviour. The Unique Group is getting the blame for a lot of things, but in some cases parks have signed up with Noel Edmonds in the hope that he's going to turn their businesses round. But it takes a darn sight more than just Noel Edmonds to do that.

'When he comes along with his nice, trite, little package, people grab it, thinking it's going to make them a great deal of money. They sign on the dotted line, thinking everything's going to be rosy. They sign a five-year contract and the first year Mr Blobby makes a bit of an impact and attendances go up. But by the following year they have gone back to where they were before, the only difference being that they now have a creditor on their list, name of Noel Edmonds. And it's damn unfortunate that if it fails he gets the blame for it because he's the last in the door.'

Pilot Ken Summers sheds further light on the problems faced by the star. Ken, who flew Noel for more than fifteen years, never experienced any difficulties with their business arrangements. 'I was involved in the first few *Garden Parties* that he did, including the original one which was televised,' he explains. 'I did get paid but I heard on the grapevine that there was a bit of a controversy with some of the other pilots who were asking for too much money and Noel wasn't very pleased about it because the whole thing was supposed to be on a charity basis. But I personally never had any hassle at all. I just put in what I wanted and got it without any problem. I've always had a very good relationship with Noel, both professionally and on a personal level.' He adds, 'A couple of people have mentioned that he uses people to get his own way, but I think that is only in the sense that he gets things done. People have to do that sometimes and I'm sure that's how he became successful.'

In the words of the company's brochure, 'Unique believes in spotting opportunities and niches where it can create or add value and moving swiftly to capitalise.' The furore over the theme parks at Bicton Park, Cricket St Thomas and Morecambe has led to unwelcome publicity for Noel and revealed a more serious side to the man we see on TV. But in Unique's defence, its chief executive, Paul Pascoe, says, 'We never profess to be expert in theme-park operations; we are experts at understanding the benefits that TV properties can bring to leisure parks. We have the benefit of Noel's publicity but the other side of the sword is that everything we do is in the public eye. I am often asked why Unique is so litigious. But we're not. It's upsetting that we've had these problems but we only litigate when we are in the right. We hate going to court and never do it unless we have to.'

Throughout this often difficult period, Noel was keeping up with the lucrative – and much less troublesome – advertising and sponsorship work that he had begun in his early days at Radio 1. Deals to promote Trebor Bassett sweets and Maxwell House coffee, and consultant work for Cellnet and British Airways bumped up his income, as did his personal appearances, for which he charged up to £25,000 a day. In March 1996 he celebrated the hundredth episode of *House Party*, a triumph over the whingers and the knockers. Noel had once again had the last laugh over the sneering telly snobs. 'What I hate is the insinuation that if you watch *House Party* you must have had a full frontal lobotomy,' he complained. 'I don't mind admitting it hurts, but I have to accept it. I'm fair game, but I don't like people who criticise the viewers. The humour isn't puerile – in some instances it's quite sophisticated. I don't believe we are cruel to people. Most NTV targets say it's one of the best things that ever happened to them. It baffles me, but some people in this country like to knock success. All I'm doing is trying to entertain people. *House Party* is a very easy target to have a go at, but at least I'm trying to do something different.'

The following month Noel picked up an early Christmas

present – an £8 million deal to stay with the BBC for another four years. *House Party* was back on top, attracting up to 13 million watchers and beating *Blind Date* once again. The 'golden handcuffs' deal made Noel Britain's highest-paid TV entertainer, but the big question on everyone's lips was, How long could he stay at the top? The next year would see him embark on his biggest gamble yet: a high-stakes game of brinkmanship that would threaten his 28-year career with the BBC. And the spectre of Michael Lush's death would return to haunt him as he dealt with another dreadful tragedy.

# 12 Highs and Lows

A FTER A QUIET and uneventful start to 1997, the year turned into arguably one of the worst of Noel's life. A series of disasters, both personal and financial, meant that he was never out of the news, and, as the year progressed, things only appeared to get worse.

In June, Noel's attempt to triumph at Le Mans, the world's most famous and glamorous motor race, ended in failure. The star's private obsession had long been to have the winning team at the arduous 24-hour endurance event, and he teamed up with American millionaire Don Panoz to sponsor an exciting, all-new, British-designed car called the Panoz GTR. Hardly anybody had heard of the Batmobile-style car, and motoring writer Jeremy Clarkson thought it the strangest entry in the entire race. 'When Noel said he wanted to set up a team that could and would win, I thought he might have lost a marble in his beard,' wrote Clarkson, who also presents BBC's *Top Gear* programme. 'People told him, "Don't do it!" Deciding you're going to run a car at Le Mans is like deciding you're going on a cycle ride to Mars – a great idea but it can't be done.' Clarkson wasn't alone in his scepticism. When Noel announced his plans to motoring journalists there were muffled guffaws deriding the chances of 'that bloke on the telly' and sarcastic suggestions that Mr Blobby wouldn't be able to fit behind the wheel of the car.

Noel was undeterred. His racing car had just achieved its maiden victory in the United States in only its third race, and he had a top team for the race. The car had a huge six-litre Ford engine capable of up to 230 mph, inspired by the legendary Ford GT40, of which Noel owns a rare 1965 version. 'I always wanted to be involved with a British team running a British-designed car at Le Mans and now we are going to do it,' said Noel. 'Le Mans is unique, gruelling and demands a huge amount from the teams. But we have a marvellous new car, great drivers, and we are serious. If I wasn't serious about winning, I wouldn't do it. But we aim to be up there – this Le Mans is going to be really special.' The preparations and the race were to be screened on TV in a two-part special, called *Noel's Le Mans Party*.

Matt James, Formula One editor for *Motoring News* magazine, says the plan was flawed from the start. 'The Panoz was the wrong sort of car for Le Mans,' he explains. 'To start with, its engine was in the front and a front-engined car hasn't won at Le Mans for thirty years. The whole concept was wrong. The car kept overheating during practice runs but they couldn't pull out of the race because they were in too deep and had already told everyone they would be competing. Everyone expected them to make a hash of it and for the car to blow up within an hour, but in fact it excelled itself and lasted for 16 hours of the 24. For a while it made it into the bottom of the top ten and it looked as if it was going to have a fairy-tale ending, but then it blew up. It was all very well intentioned but not very well executed – fancy taking over from reality.'

But a far more serious event was to overshadow that year. On 13 July 1997, a nine-year-old boy was crushed to death in a helicopter accident at an event organised by Noel's charity, Airborne. Noel was at the airshow, near the Queen Mother's childhood home, Glamis Castle in Perthshire, when the helicopter carrying Garry Malley and other special-needs children crashed in a field in driving rain. The day had started with the best intentions: to give youngsters with special needs the ride of a lifetime in a helicopter. It ended with a young boy losing his life and four other children being injured. Memories of Michael Lush's death came flooding back as the star incredulously found himself involved in another tragedy.

Noel had founded the charity in 1994 after being swamped by letters from parents asking for their children's dream to be fulfilled by a trip in his helicopter. That a child should die during something that was supposed to bring pleasure devastated him. Announcing that he was cancelling all work for the foreseeable future, he said, 'I am heartbroken that a day that offered so much happiness to so many wonderful children ended in tragedy. Everyone associated with Airborne is absolutely devastated by this. For the past four years the charity has provided helicopter rides for almost 7,000 special-needs children and our nationwide parties have been completely free of incident.'

Garry, who had minor learning difficulties, had gone along to the event with his mother Sandra and seven-year-old sister Leeanne. Since the boy's death, Noel has forged a friendship with Garry's father, Tam Simpson, which has comforted Tam enormously. 'Meeting Noel made me realise that we weren't alone in our grief,' he says. 'Celebrities seem so distant on a TV screen, but he is a very real person. He has been phoning me and helping me through what's been happening. He told me that, if I ever want to speak to anybody, I can phone him to talk.'

Noel didn't attend the funeral but sent a wreath of white carnations and yellow roses with the message: 'You will always be in our hearts and prayers for ever more, love Noel, Helen, Charlotte, Lorna and Olivia.' And shortly afterwards he went to Scotland to see Tam and Sandra. Tam says, 'He flew up to see us and we met at the Swallow Hotel. He was as shocked as we were and told us that he was pressing for a Fatal Accident Inquiry. He is on our side and we have become friends.' Noel revealed to Tam and Sandra that he had planted a tree at his home in Garry's memory, and offered to pay for the family to go on holiday. At Tam's request, Noel relaunched the charity two months after the accident. 'He said he was going to cancel Airborne as a result of Garry's death, but we begged him to keep the charity going. It's what Garry would have wanted.'

In January 1998, an Air Accident Investigation branch report blamed pilot error for the crash. A spokesman for Airborne said they were 'appalled' at the contents of the report. 'Frankly, the flight should never have taken place,' they said. 'The report reveals a lot of information that we were not aware of on the day.' Noel said he was upset that the report had taken six months to compile. 'The report is very clear and concise. As a pilot of some experience I had a pretty good idea of why the accident occurred. Now it is up to others to decide on the sort of action to be taken.' The report clearly concluded that Noel was in no way to blame, and Tam and Sandra fully agree with those findings.

After the trauma of Garry Malley's death, there was further upset for Noel when his father-in-law Dave suffered a heart attack. Noel admitted it heaped on the grief. 'It has been such a sad, sad summer. I am very close to Helen's dad and just recently I found out that a very close friend of mine at the BBC has cancer.' He added, 'Garry's death was a tragedy for everyone involved and it did make me go away and wonder if there was any point in carrying on. It was a black, black time. I'm very bad at dealing with negativity and that tragedy came out of genuinely trying to make people happy. I went through a very bad grieving period and then I had to try to look at the positive elements. Even in the darkest hour there is a glimmer. I was reduced to tears by phone calls from celebs who have supported us over the years.'

Three months after the *News of the World* story, the rumours about the state of his marriage were still annoying Noel and he was once again complaining that people were trying to stitch him up. 'Certain people would like to see me fail, but the one thing that no one is ever going to get me for is my marriage,' he said grimly. 'Nothing will get between Helen and I except death. That's why I'm such a strong individual and why I'll take on all comers in the end.'

Noel was keen to assure everyone that his marriage was in fine shape and, in an extraordinary interview with the *Daily Mail*, he spoke openly about his love life: 'In every aspect of what a man wants from a woman, I could not have found a better partner. Helen's physical attraction for me has never changed. Intimately, our relationship is better than it has ever been. I'm very possessive: she's mine – I've got a bit of paper to say I bought her. Of course we have disagreements. We're two quite forceful people. We'll say awful things to each other. But we're very quick to make up and forgive each other. I trust her, but that doesn't stop me noticing the bloke in the restaurant who has hardly eaten anything because he is staring at my wife. But, on the other hand, I love it when Helen dresses in a sexy way.'

He also revealed the lengths to which he goes to assure Helen that he's being faithful: 'Helen doesn't get jealous. When I'm not at home we talk at least five times a day on the phone and every day my office produces an itinerary with all my movements, so she knows exactly what I'm doing. I have had women openly flirting with me right in front of Helen – I was really taken aback. It's a funny thing about women that they do like to go after married men. To me, women seem terribly competitive animals. I can't imagine any set of circumstances where I would be unfaithful to Helen, or that Helen and I wouldn't be together. Please God, Helen and I do not drift apart. We have a very special relationship, the kind people find only once in a lifetime, and some people never find. I was married before for eleven years, and I know this is better. This is right.'

After a sad and frustrating 1997, there was good news in the form of a £1 million settlement from Lancaster City Council – a gratifying end to a three-year battle over the Crinkley Bottom theme park. And shortly before Christmas, Noel and Helen happily announced that she was pregnant again. Noel – ever the optimist – was still hoping for a son to play football and cricket with, but, once more, Helen presented him with a daughter. Alice, their fourth girl, was born in June 1998, weighing 7lb 8oz. A delighted Noel hired a giant billboard to celebrate her birth. As he drove Helen and the new baby home from the hospital, he took a detour into Okehampton town centre to show his wife the enormous 25ft-by-12ft hoarding. It featured a red heart and a stork delivering a baby, with the message: 'HELEN AND ALICE, WELCOME HOME!! CONGRATULATIONS AND ALL OUR LOVE, NOEL, CHARLOTTE, LORNA, OLIVIA, AND ALL AT UNIQUE GROUP.'

Family life is something that means a lot to Noel. Old videos of him from the 1970s inevitably cause a great deal of mirth in the Edmonds household. 'When Olivia was four she was watching an old *Top of the Pops* and she shouted, "Mummy, Mummy, there's a girl on the telly who looks like Daddy," ' he laughed. 'They used to like watching me on TV but I think they've got fed up of it now. She turned off *Telly Addicts* the other day and said, "There's too much Daddy on the television." And when Lorna was seven she brought a friend home and introduced her to us. She said, "This is my mummy and this is Noel Edmonds." So I asked, "Why did you call me that?" And she said, "I just thought I'd get the embarrassing bit out of the way." '

Charlotte, who turned sixteen in October 1998, is a talented horsewoman who has already made her mark riding for Britain. No one is prouder of her than Noel. 'She won a bronze medal representing Great Britain in the European Pony Championship and when she stood there as the National Anthem was played I blubbed shamelessly,' he admitted. 'I think I shed more water that night than Jacques Cousteau ever swam through. Her ambition is to ride for Britain at the next Olympics, and that is fine by me. She will get all the support that Helen and I can give her.' But when the star was asked to present the prizes at a dressage show he politely said no. 'I want Charlotte to be known on her own merits and for her own abilities, and not as Charlotte Edmonds, Noel Edmonds' daughter,' he explained. 'I go to see her ride purely and simply as a dad.'

But devoted family man is only one of the many sides to Noel Edmonds. He admits he has had to be tough to get where he is today and confesses that one of his heroes is Francis Urquart, the ruthless fictional MP of Michael Dobson's book and TV drama *House of Cards*. 'In this country, it's a fine tightrope you walk to appear successful enough that people want to associate with you, but not so successful that they loathe you,' he explained. It is something he has not always managed to pull off. He recently made it to number eighteen in the list of Britain's Fifty Most Unpopular People, sandwiched between Dale Winton and Bruce Forsyth. And, on an Internet website named Slap a Celeb, people can run their cursor over Noel's face and make his head jerk back in horror. The site has been 'hit' nearly 6,000 times.

But those who mock him fail to appreciate the steely side to his nature. Dismissing him as an object of ridicule is to seriously underestimate the power that he wields in television. As he said himself, 'I put an enormous amount of effort into what I do. I take it seriously and I wouldn't like to think that it's dismissed by everybody instantly.' He is fully prepared to put aside his Mr Nice Guy image and fight his corner if need be – as he demonstrated in January 1998 when he pulled *House Party* after that row with the BBC. Speaking two weeks after pulling off the biggest gamble of his career, the star admitted it had been a stressful battle. 'This whole episode has been a very, very unpleasant experience – one of the worst of my career,' he said. 'I knew I could be fired at any moment. It was a very dark moment but, now everything has been sorted out, I know it will never, ever happen again.'

He was right: it surely couldn't happen again. The television and media world had been incredulous that Noel had got away with it once – to attempt it twice would be unthinkable.

Explaining why he took the decision to take *House Party* off the air, he said, 'It was the first time in 29 years with the

BBC that I have failed to do a television or radio show – I had never even been ill. So that will give you an idea of my personal commitment and how seriously I took the issue. I thought it was below the standard that the light-entertainment department should accept. I couldn't present a show like that. I can't lie to the viewers and tell them we have lots of goodies on the show, when there clearly aren't. I hadn't got the confidence to go ahead with it. I simply told everyone in the team how disenchanted I was, and, when I realised everyone agreed with me but had the obligation to continue, I had to call the shots. The BBC knew there was obviously a serious problem for me to behave like that. I am no prima donna.'

Noel was triumphant in his victory, although his words would soon come back to haunt him. 'The agreement at the highest level of the BBC was that until we knew we could make high-quality shows we would have to take a break,' he said. 'The response has been: "This show is so important to us we have to get it right." They have given me a massive vote of confidence. Now I'm sure *House Party* has a great future ahead of it.' The experience had served only to strengthen his determination, he said. 'I had an incredible mailbag, which I have found very touching. You realise that for 9 or 10 million people *House Party* really is an important part of their lives. It has given me a little more self-confidence and reinforced my resolve to protect *House Party* and the things I believe in.'

But the big question on the lips of those who know the star was: Edmonds may have won the battle but would he survive to win the war? Yes and no. Noel had his enemies before at the BBC and his actions in January 1998 won him a few more. There is certainly no shortage of people waiting to gloat should he fall from grace. 'Noel is one of those people who move through life picking people up and dropping them,' says Derek James. 'Everybody has their day when they are flavour of the month, but when he's finished he dumps them like used tissues. But he is going to run out of people soon. It is just like a dam: the hole is going to get bigger and suddenly the whole thing will just go down horribly. But if it does go wrong he's only got himself to blame because of the cavalier way he treats people. He's come a long way and done very well for himself but you have to remember that, those you tread on on the way up, you might perhaps face on the way down. There seem to be quite a few of them around and it amazes me, quite frankly, how he always manages to come up smelling of roses.'

To more than a few raised eyebrows, *House Party* survived, and an all-new production team was brought in for the revamped 1998–9 series. The official line was that everyone was happy. Paul Pascoe of Unique said, 'The resources and commitment that the BBC has shown us this time have been brilliant. Noel's relationship with the BBC is better than ever.' But Noel acknowledged that his series had been under threat. 'We are a Premier League show and frankly we nearly got relegated,' he said.

But the efforts Noel had made to improve the show failed to silence the critics, who were still of the general belief that *House Party* had run its natural course. One of the much heralded new features of the show, sofa soccer, was an unmitigated disaster, with the machine shooting out footballs at such speed that even England goalkeeper David Seaman couldn't catch them. 'Clever Noel Edmonds has come up with a way for us to have a turkey all year round with *House Party*,' wrote the *Sun*'s TV critic, Garry Bushell, at Christmas. Few disagreed with him.

The average viewing figures were 7.3 million, half what they were during the show's heyday. The bad reviews were there for Noel to read week after week and he admitted to friends that he was 'up against the wall'. He has always been adamant that he will be the one who decides when to go. A perfectionist who holds a postmortem after every show, he said he would scrap *House Party* rather than see it fail. 'When it's time to go I hope I spot it before anybody else,' he said. 'I'm sure we'll stop *House Party* before it drops off the edge. I've always been one to leave the party before people start putting on their pyjamas and wishing you'd leave.'

But in the event it would not be Noel who would make the decision to scrap *House Party*, but the BBC. In February 1999 they pulled the plug when viewing figures slumped to an unacceptable 5.9 million. Announcing that the final episode would be shown on 20 March, Noel admitted it was a relief, 'I feel as if a huge weight has been lifted off my shoulders,' he said. The BBC underlined its support for the star and both they and Noel promised that he would be back in the the year 2000 with a brand new Saturday night show. Noel planned to spend the rest of 1999 working behind the scenes on a 'ground-breaking, new and exciting' show for the millennium. He managed to sound gung-ho and upbeat about it but having *House Party* axed in the very year in which he celebrates 30 years with the BBC is hardly what he would have hoped for. At the time of writing, Noel is at something of a cross-roads in his professional life and the pressure is on him now more than ever before. How he copes with this latest set-back will be hugely important. Those who know and work with him say that as the heat is turned up, the more uncompromising and determined he becomes. It is clear that Noel felt he – and *House Party* – were unfairly attacked and that is something that caused him genuine grief. Not being able to do much about it makes him feel impotent, for what riles Edmonds more than anything is not having control over something. As one television writer remarks, 'Edmonds is pleasant and charming when things are going well for him and his shows are high in the ratings, but he can't take criticism. The fact that he has no control over what people write about him makes him furious, and he can be very spiteful and vengeful when it suits him.'

Critics who used to enjoy a friendly relationship with the star now find themselves *persona non grata*: just some of the many people who have come and gone in Noel's life during his thirty-year career in show business. The people that still figure prominently number far fewer, but include Michael Hurll and Michael Leggo. Hurll has worked with the star for more than 22 years. He was the producer on *The Late, Late Breakfast Show* and the two have remained close. Unique Television took Michael Hurll Television under its wing and they are working on projects together. Michael Leggo, whom Noel has known for nearly as long, devised *House Party* with him and produced the show until he became Head of Light Entertainment at the BBC. Describing the star's unique appeal, Leggo said, 'Noel has that boy-next-door charm. The viewer knows that they will be taken on an entertaining journey but that he will deliver them safely back to their homes. Noel is unpretentious, unselfish, never greedy for laughs.' Mike Smith, whose friendship with Noel didn't survive so well, disagrees. Smith believes that the star works best when he's hosting a one-man show such as *House Party*. 'He's much better on his own,' he says. 'Because he is, in the nicest sense of the word, selfish.'

Noel has undoubtedly come a long way on the route from Gidea Park to Crinkley Bottom, and his position as multimillionaire and one of the top entertainers in television still amazes some of his old friends and acquaintances. 'I knew he was ambitious but I never thought he would go on to be quite so successful – his business acumen is really extraordinary,' says David Jensen. 'Noel is a difficult guy to get to know. I think he's probably guarded because, when people have a big profile like he has, and it's known that they have a lot of money, he may be suspicious of people's motives. He is obviously quite an influential wheeler dealer in show business.'

But, regardless of his success, Noel remains somehow insecure and it is this that is his Achilles heel. You don't have to scrape away too much of the adult Noel to find the scholarship boy who nervously arrived at Brentwood School with something to prove. Despite his vast wealth and the trappings of his success, he appears at times to have an almost desperate need to prove himself.

He remains remarkably sensitive to criticism and has more than once been accused of petulance. He is prickly and defensive of any negative remarks made about himself or his show, when other famous people learnt to take such things in their stride years ago. This is illustrated by the fact that he is still haunted by the time, more than twenty years ago, when he was referred to as 'chillingly ambitious'. 'I'm not a chillingly ambitious man,' he insisted. 'I have never wanted success at all costs. The only trouble is that in this country they build you up to knock you down. No one's managed to so far – but there may be someone round the corner. I've just made the best of everything that's come my way. I want my kids to learn that lesson and I tell them, "Don't squander your chances: when an opportunity knocks, grab it with both hands."

'I have had to pinch myself sometimes, not least because of the fact that I was born in Essex. I've tiptoed through minefields and survived. If I had any advice to give to someone starting out in the business I would have to say, "Be true to yourself, be professional, and have a conscience. If you do achieve a certain wealth and position, don't let it get to you." '

Whatever the future holds, Noel's position as a key player in mainstream TV is assured. For as long as television seeks to woo Joe Public on a Saturday night, there will be a place at the top table for Noel Edmonds.